NUGGETS OF THE NEW THOUGHT

SEVERAL THINGS THAT HAVE HELPED PEOPLE

WILLIAM WALKER ATKINSON

TRUE SIGN
PUBLISHING HOUSE

Published by True Sign Publishing House
Address: SY. No. 21/2 & 21/3, Sonnenahalli,
Krishnarajapura, Bengaluru,
Karnataka - 560049 India
E-mail: truesignbooks@gmail.com
Website: www.truesign.in

Nuggets of The New Thought
Several Things That Have Helped People
Author: William Walker Atkinson

ISBN: 978-93-5584-025-7

First Edition: 2022

Contents

Preface

I do not like writing a preface—it seems too much like an apology. I have no special apology to tender for offering this collection of New Thought nuggets. They may possess no literary merit, but they have *helped* men and women. With the exception of "The Secret of the I Am," these essays appeared from month to month in "New Thought," of which magazine I am associate editor. They were written hastily, principally upon the demand of the printer for "copy," and, for the most part, were printed just as they were written, there being no time for revision or polishing up. You may pick up any one of them and find many sentences needing straightening out—many thoughts which could be better expressed by the change of a few words. Knowing these things, I first thought that I would go over each essay and add a little here, and take away a little there, polishing up and burnishing as I went along. But when I looked over them, my heart failed me. There they were just as they were written—just as they were dug out of my mind—and I hadn't the heart to change them. I remembered the circumstances surrounding the writing of every one of them, and I let them alone. A "nugget" polished up would be no longer a nugget. And these thoughts are nuggets—I dug them myself. I will not say much regarding the quality of the metal—that is for you—but you see them just as they came from the mine—rough, unpolished, mixed with the rock, queerly shaped. If you think that they contain metal of sufficiently good quality, refine them, melt them and fashion them into something useful or ornamental. For myself, I like things with the bark on—with the marks of the hammer—with the original quartz adhering to the metal. But others are of different taste—they like everything to feel smooth to the touch. They will not like these nuggets. Alas, I cannot help it—I cannot produce the beautifully finished article—I have nothing to offer other than the crude product of the mine. Here they are, polish them up yourself if you prefer them in that shape—I will not touch them.

W. W. A.

Chicago, October 2, 1902.

The Keynote

"I Can and I Will"—The recognition—Equal to any task—A feeling of calm confidence—An abiding sense of power, reserve force and security —The Something within—The triple key to the door of attainment—The vibrations of Success.

"I Can and I Will!!!" Have you ever said these words to yourself with a firm conviction that you were speaking the truth—with the strong feeling that needed no other proof. If so, you then felt within you a thrill which seemed to cause every atom of your being to vibrate in harmony with some note in the grand scale of Life, sounded by the Real Self. You caught a momentary glimpse of the Inner Light—heard a stray note of the Song of the Soul—were conscious for the moment of YOURSELF. And in that moment of ecstasy you knew that untold power and possibilities were yours. You felt that you were in touch with all Strength, Power, Knowledge, Happiness and Peace. You felt that you were equal to any task—capable of executing any undertaking. For the moment there was no Fear in the world for you. All the Universe seemed to vibrate in the same key with your thought. For the moment you RECOGNIZED THE TRUTH.

But alas, the spirit of doubt, distrust, fear and unfaith called you again to Earth—and the vision faded. And yet, the remembrance of the sight—the echo of the sound—the remnant of the new-found strength—is with you still. You still find that memory to be a stimulus to great efforts—a comforting thought in times of weakness and trial. You have been able to accomplish much by the aid of the lingering vibrations of the mighty thought.

In times of great peril—grave perplexities—life and death struggles, a feeling of calm confidence and strength often comes to us, and we are borne on by a power *of* us and *in* us (and yet in everything else, too) that seems to lift us off our feet and sweep us on to safety—to peace—to rest. We are possessed of an abiding sense of power, reserve force and security. When extraordinary conditions confront us—when our bodies seem paralyzed—our minds stupefied—our will power gone, we are often made conscious of the existence of the Real Self, and it answers our involuntary demand, and comes to rescue with the cheering cry: "I AM HERE"!

Many of us have made use of this inner strength without realizing it. One day we were sorely distressed and made the demand, and lo! it was answered. We knew not from whence came this new-found strength, but we were conscious of the uplift, and felt more confidence in ourselves. The next time we *confidently* demanded the aid, and again we were answered. We acquired that which we call confidence and faith in ourselves, and were carried over many a dark place and started on the road to Success. Our repeated success caused us to think and speak of our "luck," and we grew to believe that we had a "star," and took chances and risks that others would not dream of. We dared. We made some apparent failures, but we soon came to know them as only lessons leading to *ultimate* success. The "I Can and I Will" feeling carried us over rough places safely, and we got to simply *know* that we would "get there" in the end.

And so we went on and on, knowing that if we advanced three steps and slipped back two, we were still one step ahead. We had confidence, because we *knew* that "things would come our way" in the end. And so long as we held this attitude, we *did* succeed, and it was only when we lost heart at some unexpected slip—only when, after having attained success, we became dazed and frightened, and began to fear that our "luck might turn" and that we would lose all of our accumulations—it was only *then*, I say—that our star waned.

Talk with any successful man, and, if truthful, he will admit having felt, from the time of his first success, that he had some sort of "pull" with Fate—some "lucky star"—some special Providence operating in his behalf. He grew to *expect* results—to have confidence in things turning out right—to have faith in *something* of which he knew not the nature—and he was not disappointed. Things seemed to work in his favor—not always just in the way he expected, sometimes in an entirely different way—matters seemed somehow to straighten themselves out in the end—so long as he kept his "nerve." He did not know the source of his strength, but he believed in it and trusted it just the same.

Let us wake up and recognize this Something Within—let us begin to understand this "I Can and I Will" feeling—let us cherish it if we have it, and cultivate it if we have it not. Do you know that we are young giants who have not discovered our own strength? Are you not aware that there are powers latent within us, pressing forth for development and unfoldment? Do you not know that earnest desire, faith and calm demand will bring to us that which we require—will place at our hand the tools with which we are to work out our destiny—will guide us in the proper use of the tools—will make us grow? Do you not know that Desire, Faith and Work is the triple key to the doors of Attainment? There are possibilities before us, awaiting our coming, of which we have never dreamed. Let us assert ourselves—take up the key—unlock the doors—and enter our kingdom.

To accomplish, we must be possessed of earnest desire—must be as confident of ultimate success as we are of the rising of to-morrow's sun—we must have Faith. And we must work out the end with the tools and instruments that will present themselves day by day. We will find that Desire, Confidence, Faith and Work will not only brush aside the obstacles from our path, but will also begin to assert that wonderful force, as yet so little understood—the Law of Attraction—which will draw to us that which is conducive to our success, be it ideas, people, things, yes, even *circumstances*. Oh, ye of little Faith, why do you not see these things?

The world is looking for these "I Can and I Will" people—it has places ready for them—the supply does not begin to equal the demand. Pluck up courage ye unfortunate ones—ye doubters—ye "I Can't" people! Begin the fight by abolishing Fear from your minds. Then start to climb the ladder of Attainment, shouting "I CAN AND I WILL" with all your might, drowning out the sound of the "buts," "ifs," "supposings," "you can'ts" and "aren't you afraids" of your wet-blanket friends at the foot of the ladder. Do not bother about the upper rounds of the ladder—you will reach them in time—but give your whole attention to the round just ahead of you, and when you have gained a firm footing on that, then look at the next one. One round at a time, remember, and *give your entire attention to each step*. Climb with Desire, Confidence and Faith inspiring each step, and the task will become a pleasure. You will be conscious of some mighty force attracting you upward and onward as you progress. And don't try to pull some other fellow off the ladder—there's room enough for both of you—be kind, be kind.

If you fail to feel the "I Can and I Will" vibrations within you, start in to-day, and *say* "I Can and I Will"—THINK "I Can and I Will"—ACT "I Can and I Will," and get the vibrations started in motion. Remember that as the one note of the violin, if constantly sounded, will cause the mighty bridge to vibrate in unison so will one positive thought, held constantly, manifest itself both in yourself, others and things. So begin sounding the note to-day—this very moment. Sound it constantly. Send forth a clear, glad, joyous note—a note of Faith—a note of coming Victory. Sound it over and over again, and soon you will become conscious that the vibrations have commenced, and that the mighty structure of your being is quivering and vibrating to the keynote:—"I CAN AND I WILL."

The Secret of The "I Am"

> The Ego—The physical plane—The mental plane—The new plane of consciousness—The Real Self—The "I"—The Temple of the Living Spirit—Development of the "I Am" consciousness—The Higher Reason.

"Lord of a thousand worlds am I,
    And I reign since time began;
And Night and Day in cyclic sway,
    Shall pass while their deeds I scan.
Yet time shall cease, ere I find release,
    FOR I AM THE SOUL OF MAN."

—Charles H. Orr.

Many of us are accustomed to thinking of ourselves on the physical plane alone. When we think of the Ego—the "I" of ourselves, we picture it as a human body with organs ranging from the finest—the brain, down to those of coarser atomic structure. To one living on this plane of consciousness the body is the *real* self, and the Mind but an appendage to the body. Such a man speaks of "my mind" or "my soul," as he speaks of "my hat," "my coat," "my shoes"—as things belonging to him, which he uses, but which are not *him*. To him the Body is the real man—the Mind something useful to the body—the Spirit a nebulous hypothetical something of which he has but a hazy idea and no consciousness. He lives on the physical plane alone.

Others picture their "I" as Intellect or Mind, having control of the body and its organs, and having its abode in the brain, or brains, of the human being. To these people the Intellect is the Real Self, in fact to many of this class the Intellect is elevated to the position of God, and they bow down to and worship it. They realize the subjection of the body to the Mind, and are aware of the wonderful power of the latter over the particular body under its control; the bodies of others; the minds of others. To them the

Intellect is the highest self, identical with the Spirit. They are conscious of the wonderful workings of the mind, but are conscious of nothing higher. To some of them death seems to end all, their idea of mind being that it is a product of the brain. Others feel that somehow, somewhere, their Intellect will maintain its existence, but it is merely a *belief* or hope, based upon the words of others who have claimed authority to speak. They have no consciousness of pre-existence or future existence—no perception of that REAL SELF which *knows* itself to be Eternal.

A third class have so far progressed along the Path of Life that they have crossed the borders of a new plane of consciousness. They are in a strange land—they see no familiar landmarks—they do not recognize the country that lies before them. Their friends, whom they have left just a few feet behind across the border, do not seem to realize the difference the short distance has made to those who have traveled it, and therefore doubt the prospect seen from the new point of view. Those who have crossed the border find that they have acquired a *consciousness* of a real Existence. The "I" consciousness has passed beyond the Intellectual plane and is able to look back to that plane and the one still further back, the Physical plane. "I" recognizes the value of both Mind and Body, but regards them both as but instruments, tools or servants, with which to work. "I" feels that it has existed from the beginning (if beginning there was) and will exist until the end (if end there be). "I" feels a keen pleasure in mere existence—in the NOW. "I" knows itself to be a part of the WHOLE THING—knows that the UNIVERSE is its home. "I" knows itself to be a tiny drop of Spirit from the Great Spirit Ocean; a ray from the Supreme Sun; a particle of the Divine Being, encased in a material body, using that body and a force called Mind, with which to manifest itself. "I" does not at present *understand* all things—far from it. It has not as yet been able to bring its tools to that degree of perfection. It merely *knows* that it IS, and has ALWAYS BEEN, and ALWAYS WILL BE. "I" allows Intellect to indulge in speculations, but contents itself with the knowledge that it IS—it frets not itself with the problems of the past or future, but lives in the NOW, and knows itself to be a part of the WHOLE. "I" knows that it cannot be destroyed or injured—that it exists in accordance with Law (and that Law is Good) and asks no further light at this time, knowing that in its progress through matter, discarding sheath after sheath, more *knowing* will surely come. It says trustfully and confidently, to the Absolute: "Thy Will be Done."

Knowing itself to be immortal, "I" has no fear of the death of the body—one body is as good as another to it—it is willing to lay aside the body as it does a coat, when it has outworn or outgrown it. Knowing itself to be impregnable to harm, "I" has no Fearthought—it fears nothing. Knowing that the Law is working for development (always for ultimate good) "I" is not disturbed by the cares, troubles and sorrows of Life—it knows them for what they are. The body may be in pain, the mind may be burdened with sorrow, but "I," *knowing*, smiles.

"I" knows itself to be One with the "I" of all living creatures, and knowing this cannot manifest Hate, Fear, Envy, Jealousy—it cannot Despise or Condemn. These and other feelings of the old life drop from the person like a discarded mantle when "I" mounts its throne. "I" recognizes that others may not have progressed so far on the path as itself, but knows them to be but fellow travelers on the same road, who are doing the best they know how, considering their stage of the journey. "I" recognizes Ignorance—not Evil. "I" has but one feeling toward Mankind and the whole living world—LOVE. Aye, Love and Comradeship for even the *last man*, for it knows that that last man cannot be left out of the great scheme of Life.

"I" knows that it has traveled a long road leading to its present position, and that all Life is traveling the same. "I" looks back and sees others covered with the mire and dust of the road, far back on the Path, but knowing that it has traveled the same stage of the journey—been covered with the same mire and mud—it cannot condemn. "I" knows that it is but on the threshold of the new consciousness—the borderland of the Cosmic Knowing—and that far beyond lie regions of marvelous beauty which will in turn be traveled, and then on and on, increasing in strength and knowing-power each day. "I" sees endless phases of existence opening up to the vision—it cannot at this time *understand*, but it knows of the existence of the Law, and is content. "I" has the courage of Intelligent Faith, and presses forward cheerfully to the Divine Adventure. All this—and more.

To the man or woman who understands, the task of self-development becomes a labor of love—an exalted task rather than the mere selfish striving after power. As the sculptor saw in the block of marble the form of the angel, and was impelled to cut away the surrounding material in order to liberate the angelic form—so may we, seeing the God-like form within us, strive to liberate it. That inner form is the real self—the "I." If you have never realized this truth, relax body and mind and indulge in a little introspection; turn your gaze inward; listen to the voice of the Spirit. You will be conscious of a faint recognition of the Something Within striving to make itself manifest to your understanding—asking for the proper tools with which to work. Listen, listen in The Silence! Day by day the Voice will grow plainer—day by day the Light will grow brighter—your own is coming to you, at last. O, joy unspeakable! O tears! O laughter! After long ages you are coming in sight of the Promised Land.

Know yourself O Man! Know that you have within you the Divine Spark, to which both body and mind are but servants. Know that your body is the Temple of the Living Spirit and respect it as such. Know that your Intellect is but the instrument of the manifestation of the Spirit—the "I."

Do not crawl on your belly like a worm; do not humble yourself in the dust and call upon heaven to witness what a despicable creature you are; do not call yourself a miserable sinner worthy only of eternal damnation. No! a thousand times No! Rise to your feet; raise your head; face the skies; throw back your shoulders; fill your lungs with Nature's ozone. Then say to yourself: "I AM."

Man has acquired a wonderful power when he can *understandingly* say: "I AM a part of the Eternal Life Principle; I AM created in the Divine Image; I AM filled with the Divine Breath of Life; Nothing can hurt ME, for I AM ETERNAL."

The first requisite for the acquirement of an understanding of the Law is the recognition of the existence and the power of the Real Self—the "I." The more complete the recognition the greater the power. Special directions for the acquirement of this faculty of recognition cannot be given. It must be grown into and felt, rather than reasoned out by the Intellect. You will not be long in doubt as to whether or not you are on the right track; if you are right you will begin to realize it at once. You will have glimpses of it, and then it may slip away from you for a while, but fear not, you cannot escape it in the end.

You will feel that your body is but as a garment which whilst covering you temporarily is not YOU. You will feel that you are separate and apart from your body, although for a time living in it. You will feel that you could as well live in some other body, and still retain your sense of individuality. You will realize then even your mind is not You, but is merely the instrument through which You manifest yourself, and which being imperfect prevents the complete expression of the Spirit. In short, when you say, or think, "I AM," you are conscious of the existence of your *real* self, and feel the growth of a new sense of power within you. This recognition of the self may be faint, but encourage it and it will grow, and whilst growing will manifest itself to your mind by impressing upon the latter the knowledge of the proper plan for further development. It is another example of "to him that hath shall be given."

This mere calling of their attention to the fact will awaken the first glimmer of recognition in some; others will find it necessary to reflect upon the idea and awaken to a recognition of the Truth more slowly. Some will not *feel* the Truth. To such I say: The time is not yet ripe for your recognition of this great Truth, but the seed is planted and the plant will appear in time. This may seem like the veriest nonsense to you now, but the time will come when you will admit its literal correctness. You will find that a desire has been created that will cause a mental unrest until more light is received. As Walt Whitman says: "My words will itch in your ears till you understand them." As Emerson says: "You cannot escape from your good." To those who feel the first indications of the awakening of the Spirit, I say: Carry the thought with you and it will unfold like the lotus, naturally and gradually; the truth once recognized cannot be lost, and there is no standing still in nature.

What has been said is but a faint hint of a mighty Truth, which nestles in the bosom of the esoteric teachings of all religions—in the philosophies of the Orient and of ancient Greece. You will find it in the songs of the poets—in the writings of the mystics. The advanced science of this age touches it without recognizing it fully. It is not a thing that can well be conveyed by words—it is not easily comprehended by purely intellectual processes—it must be *felt* and lived out by those who are ready for it—those for whom the time has come. It has been known to the Few throughout all ages and in all times. All races have known it. It has been handed down from teacher to pupil from the earliest days. It is that Truth which Edward Carpenter refers to when he says:

"O, let not the flame die out! Cherished age after age in its dark caverns, in its holy temples cherished. Fed by pure ministers of love—let not the flame die out."

It is difficult to convey even a hint of this Truth to any but those who are prepared to receive it. To others it will seem to be arrant folly. As Emerson says: "Every man's words, who speaks from that life, must sound vain to those who do not dwell in the same thought on their own part. I dare not speak for it. My words do not carry its august sense; they fall short and cold. Only itself can inspire whom it will * * * * Yet I desire even by profane words, if sacred I may not use, to indicate the heaven of this deity, and to report what hints I have collected of the transcendent simplicity and energy of the Highest Law."

If you prefer to try to solve the Problem of Life—the Riddle of the Universe—by scientific investigation, by exact reasoning, formal thought, mathematical demonstration—by all means follow this method. You will be taught the lesson of the power and the limitations of the human intellect. And after you have traveled round and round the circle of thought and find that you are but covering the same ground over and over again—after you have run into the intellectual *cul de sac*, the blind alley of Logic—after you have beaten your wings against the cage of the Unknowable and fall exhausted and bruised—after you have done all these things and have learned your lesson—then listen to the voice within, see the tiny flame which burns steadily and cannot be extinguished, feel the pressure of the Something Within *and let it unfold.* You will then begin to understand that as the mind of Man developed by slow stages from mere sensation to simple consciousness; from simple consciousness to self-consciousness (in its lower and higher degrees) so is there a consciousness, higher than we have heretofore imagined, in store for Man, which is even now beginning to manifest itself. You may then understand that there may be an Intelligent Faith which *knows*, not simply believes. These and other lessons you will learn in time. And when you have reached the stage where you *feel* the promptings of the Higher Reason, and live in accordance therewith, you will say with Carpenter:

"Lo! the healing power descending from within, calming the enfevered mind, spreading peace among the grieving nerves. Lo! the eternal saviour, the sought after of all the world, dwelling hidden (to be disclosed) within each * * * * O joy insuperable."

"Let A Little Sunshine In"

The young people's song—Good "New Thought" doctrine—Plenty of sunshine in life, if you look for it—Don't make a dark dungeon of your mind—Throw open the windows of your soul—How to let a little sunshine in.

The other night, just as I was dropping off to sleep, a crowd of young people passed along, returning from some social gathering. They were bubbling over with mirth and joy, and every girl seemed to be talking at the same time, the voices of the young men serving merely to punctuate the sentences of their fair companions. Just after they passed my window, some one started up a song, and the rest joined in. I do not know the song they sang, but the chorus went something like this:

"Let a little sunshine in;
Let a little sunshine in;
Open wide the windows,
Open wide the doors,
And let a little sunshine in."

I listened with pleasure to the words and cheerful air of the song and said to myself: "Well, that's good enough 'New Thought' doctrine for me."

The young people went on their way singing. I, now wide awake, listened and thought. The song grew fainter and fainter as the distance between us grew greater, and at last I could not clearly distinguish the words they sang, but the faint vibrations of the tune still reached me, and I imagined that I could just hear the last words of the refrain:

"Let a little Sunshine in."

Oh, if only those young people—and all young people—and all people young or old—would take to their hearts these words, and "let a little sunshine in." It is not sufficient that you merely agree that the advice is good—that you merely repeat the words mechanically—you must make thought take form in action, and not only say the words—not only think them—but you must ACT them. Make them a part of your life—incorporate the idea in your being—train yourself into the habit of opening yourself to the sunshine of Life—get into the way of letting it flow in.

"Let a little Sunshine in."

There is plenty of sunshine in life, if you only look for it. And there is plenty of shadow in life, if you only look for it. But in the things that seem all shadow to others, you will be able to find the sunshine if you but train yourself to always look for it. And in that which may seem bright sunshine to some, others will find nothing but shade—they are troubled with a mental cataract that shuts out all the rays of the sunshine of life.

"Let a little Sunshine in."

And when you learn to love the sunshine and look forward to seeing it always, you seem to draw it to you. The Law of Attraction brings to you your share of the sunshine with which the world is plentifully supplied. And, if you fall into the habit of looking for and expecting the shadow, the shadow will always be found.

"Let a little Sunshine in."

It is astonishing what a change the Mental Attitude of the person will make. Change your Mental Attitude, and the whole world seems to change. It is like taking off the smoked glasses that have caused the world to seem dark and gloomy, and seeing the brightness and colors of the world.

"Let a little Sunshine in."

Many of you have been making dark dungeons of your minds. You have steadily shut out the sun, and your minds have become musty, damp and mildewed. Across the floor crawl noxious creatures. The slimy form of Fear drags itself slowly along, leaving its track behind; the hideous shape of Jealousy eyes you from one corner—a creature of darkness; the venomous reptile Hate shows its fangs; the vampire Worry flits across the chamber. Fearful shapes are there glowering in the darkness—frightful forms crouch in corners and recesses. All is gloom, darkness, horror. A fit breeding place for the foul creatures who fear the light—a fit nursery for monsters. Look within the dark chambers of your mind—see what it really is—see what it generates. Look within—look within. Ah, you see at last. No wonder you shriek with terror—no wonder you turn away with horror. No, no, do not turn away—look and see yourself as you are. You need the lesson. Now that you see what you have been carrying around with you, and are sickened at the sight, start to work to remedy the evil. Throw wide open the doors; throw open the windows of the soul.

"Let a little Sunshine in."

Ah, yes, never fear, there is plenty of sunshine in the Universe. Plenty for all of you. There is an infinite supply. Draw it to you. Take it freely. It is there for *you*. It is your own—your very own. It is as free as air and the material sunshine. There is no tariff on it. It is not controlled by any trust or combine. It is not adulterated. It is everywhere, everywhere. Ho! ye who are dwelling in darkness! Here is Life and Happiness for you! Here is Peace for you! Here is Joy for you! Joy, comrades, Joy! Open wide your windows; open wide your doors.

"Let a little Sunshine in."

Yes, yes! I hear you say that you cannot dispel the gloom with which you are surrounded. Nonsense. Do you not know that darkness is not a positive thing—it is the essence of negation. It is not a real thing at all—it is merely the absence of light. And here you have been for all these years, believing that the darkness was a real thing that you could not get rid of. Just stop for a moment and think. If a room in your house is dark and gloomy, do you hire a man to shovel out the darkness—do you attempt to do it yourself in your desire for light? No, no, of course you do not. You just raise the shades, and throw open the shutters and the sunshine pours in and lo! the darkness has vanished. So it is with the gloom of the soul, the darkness of the mind. It is a waste of energy to attempt to dig away the darkness—to cast out the shadows. You'll never get light in that way. All that you need to do is to recognize the advantage of light—the fact that light is to be had—that there is plenty of it anxiously waiting to be let in. Then all that you need to do is to

"Let a little sunshine in;
    Let a little sunshine in;
Open wide the windows,
    Open wide the doors,
And let a little sunshine in."

The Hunger of The Soul

The soul, as well as the body and mind, requires nourishment—The want, a promise of the fulfillment—The law of unfoldment—Nourishment provided when it is needed—Provided for in the Divine Plan—The feast of good things.

The Soul, as well as the body and the mind, requires nourishment. We have felt that hunger for spiritual knowledge which transcended our hunger for bread—exceeded our craving for mental sustenance. We have felt soul-hungry and knew not with what to appease it. The Soul has cried out for food. It has been fed upon the husks of the physical plane for so long that it is fairly starving for the proper nourishment. It seeks this way and that way for the Bread of Life and finds it not. It has asked this authority and that authority for information as to where this food may be had—where could be obtained the food that would nourish the Soul—but it has been given nothing but the stone of Dogma and Creeds. At last it sank exhausted and felt that perhaps there was no bread to be had. It has felt faint and weary and almost believed that all was a delusion and a will-o'-the-wisp of the mind—that there was no reality to it. It felt the chill of despair creeping over it and all seemed lost.

But we must not lose sight of the fact that just as the hunger of the body implies that somewhere in the world is to be found that which will satisfy it—that just as the hunger of the mind implies that somewhere is to be found mental nourishment—so the mere fact that this soul-hunger *exists* is a proof that somewhere there is to be found that which the Absolute has intended to satisfy it. The *want* is the prophecy of the fulfillment. Yes, and the want and its recognition afford the means of obtaining that which will satisfy the want. When, in the course of unfoldment either on the physical, mental or spiritual plane, it becomes necessary for the well-being of the unfolding Ego to draw to itself certain things which it requires in the process of evolution, the first step toward the obtaining of that necessary thing is the consciousness of a great and pressing want—the birth of a strong desire. And then the desire grows stronger and stronger, until the

Ego becomes desperate and determines to obtain the necessary thing at any cost. The obtaining of that thing becomes the prime object in life. Students of evolution realize this fact perhaps more than the rest of us. The subconsciousness of the plant or animal becomes surcharged with this great desire, and all the conscious and subconscious power of the living thing is put forth to obtain that which is necessary for its development.

And on the mental plane the same thing is true. The hunger for knowledge, when it once possesses a man, will cause him to cut loose from old environments, surroundings and everything else which has held him, and he forces himself to the place where that knowledge may be obtained—and he obtains it. If he only wants it hard enough he gets it. When we think of Lincoln in his boyhood days, painfully and laboriously striving for knowledge, lying on his side before the log fire and reading his book by the light of its flames—and this after a hard day's work such as only the boy on the farm knows—when we think of this we may understand the effects of a strong desire possessing the mind of man or boy, woman or girl.

And this hunger for spiritual knowledge and growth, from whence comes it? When we understand the laws of spiritual unfoldment we begin to understand that the Ego is growing and developing—unfolding and casting off old worn-out sheaths. It is calling into operation new faculties—exploring new regions of the mind. In the super-conscious regions of the Soul are many faculties lying dormant, awaiting the evolutionary hour of manifestation along conscious lines. As the faculties approach the hour of birth into the new plane they manifest an uneasiness which is communicated to the subconscious and conscious planes of the mind, causing a restlessness and uneasiness which is quite disturbing to the individual in whom they are manifesting. There is a straining for expression—a reaching forward for development—a desire for growth which produces something akin to pain. All growth and development is accompanied by more or less pain. We speak of the beautiful growth of the plant—of the lily—and wish that we could grow as easily and as painlessly as it does. But we forget that *all* growth means a breaking down—a tearing away—as well as a building up and adding to. The lily's growth appears painless to us, but if we were endowed with keen enough vision—with clear enough sight—with a power enabling us to feel that which is going on within its organism, we would be made aware that there is a constant change going on—a tearing down of tissue, a using up of cells, a pressing upon and breaking through of confining sheaths—all meaning growth, development and unfoldment. We see only the birth of the new parts and lose sight of the pain and destruction preceding it. All through life is manifested the "growing pains" of development. All birth is attended with pain.

And so it is with the birth into consciousness of these unfolding spiritual faculties. We feel an uneasiness, dissatisfaction, yea, even pain, as we strive to call into conscious life these children of the Soul. We feel that desire for something needed by our inner self and we seek for it in all directions. We exhaust all of the pleasures of life, so-called, and find no satisfaction there. We then endeavor to find comfort and solace in intellectual pursuits, but without obtaining that which we seek. We pore over the writing of the philosophers and learned writers of the past and present, but find them as but husks to the hungering soul. We seek in creeds and dogmas that comforting something, the need of which we feel, but of the nature of which we are ignorant—but we find no satisfaction there. We, perhaps, go from creed to creed, from philosophy to philosophy, from one scientific theory to another scientific theory, but still we hunger. At last we get to a position in which we feel that life is not worth the living and that all is a ghastly mockery. And so we go on and on, seeking—ever seeking—but the quest is fruitless.

Man on the physical plane has a comparatively easy time of it. He lives as does the animal—he thinks as does the animal—he dies as does the animal. The problems of life fret him not. He does not even know of the existence of the problems of life. He is happy in his way, and it almost seems a pity that he must be disturbed from his state of animal content. But he *must* be disturbed, not by you or by me perhaps, but by the inevitable Law, which is working around and about him, and in him. Sooner or later in the course of his development he must be awakened. And he awakens upon the mental plane, and here his troubles begin. On the mental plane everything seems beautiful for a time. Man finds himself a new being and he goes on and on, feeling himself a very god and reveling in his intellectual powers. But after a time these things cease to satisfy him. The unfolding of the higher faculties begin to annoy him, particularly as he cannot explain them. His intellectual training has perhaps taught him to believe that there was nothing higher than the mind—that religious feelings were nothing but the result of the emotional nature and that he had outgrown all that. But still he feels that Something Within, never ceasing to annoy him—never ceasing to intrude upon his intellectual consciousness certain *feelings* entirely contrary to his theories. He has grown to doubt the existence of a Supreme Being, and having read Haekel's "Riddle of the Universe" feels that the question has been satisfactorily settled for all time, and that the answer to all of life's problems may be found in the tenets of his creed—Materialism.

But, somehow, he is not at ease. He feels the pressure of the growing Something Within and becomes quite restless. This goes on from time to time and he seeks the Truth in all directions, rushing from one thing to another in his desire to satisfy the cravings of the Soul, but all the time denying that there is anything to be found. After a time he becomes aware of a new state of consciousness developing within him, and in spite of his mental revolts against any good thing coming from within, he is forced to accept himself in his growing state, and to realize that he may possess a Knowing other than that of the intellect. It may take him a long time to accept this, but so long as he rebels against it and struggles, so long will he feel pain. And only when he catches a glimpse of the true state of affairs does he open himself up to the Divine Unfoldment going on in his Soul, and joyfully welcome the tearing away of confining mental sheaths, which destruction enables the newly born faculty to force its way into the conscious mentality. He learns to even aid in the unfoldment by holding the thoughts conducive to spiritual development, and thus assists in the bringing forth of the new leaf or flower of the Soul. It has always been so. Man has gone through stage after stage of unfoldment, suffering pain each time as the old sheaths are burst asunder and discarded. He is prone to hold on to the old sheaths and to cherish them long after they have served their purpose in his growth. And it is only when he has reached the stage that many men are now coming into a knowledge of that he understands the process of growth and is willing and glad to aid in the development instead of attempting to oppose it. He falls in with the workings of the Law instead of trying to defeat it.

Life is motion. We are moving onward and upward throughout the ages. Man has passed over miles of The Path, but he will have to travel many more before he sees the reason of the journey. But he has now reached the stage where he may see that it all means something—all is a part of a mighty plan—that this is a necessary stage of the journey, and that around the bend of the road are to be found shady trees, and a brook at which he may quench his thirst and wash away the dust of the last few miles.

This hunger of the Soul is a real thing. Do not imagine that it is an illusion—do not endeavor to deny it. If you feel it you may rest assured that your time is coming, and that there will be provided that which will satisfy it. Do not waste your energy in running hither and thither seeking for bread. The bread will be provided when it is most needed. There is no such thing in Life as spiritual starvation. But instead of seeking without for that which will nourish you, look within. At each stage of the journey the traveler will find enough to nourish him for the hour—enough to sustain him until he reaches the next stage. You cannot be denied this nourishment. It is part of the Divine Plan that it be provided for you. If you will look for it in the right place you will always find it, and will be saved much seeking and worrying. Do not be impatient because the feast is not set before you at this stage. Be satisfied with that which is given, for it suffices your needs at the present moment. By and by you will reach the stage when the feast of good things will have been earned, and you will be invited to feast and rest until you are ready for the next stage of the journey.

The great spiritual wave which is now sweeping over the world brings with it great wants, but it also carries with it the means of satisfying those wants. Do not despair.

Look Aloft!

The old sailor's advice—The warning cry—Peace and content—Mental balance recovered—The glory of the Universe—All governed by Law—The Law manifests everywhere—A reverent feeling of calm, peaceful faith—Look aloft.

I recently heard a little tale about a boy who went to sea, in the old days of the sailing vessel. One day he was ordered to go aloft, and was urged on until he reached the highest possible point on the mast. When he found that he could go no farther, he glanced down. The sight terrified him and almost caused him to lose his grip and fall headlong on the deck, far below. He felt dizzy and sick, and it seemed almost impossible for him to maintain his hold on the mast. Far below was the deck, looking so small as compared to the wide expanse of water on all sides of it. The motion made him feel as if he was suspended between heaven and earth, with nothing substantial to support him. He felt his brain reeling and his senses leaving him, and all seemed lost, when far away from the deck below, he heard an old sailor cry, "Look aloft, lad! Look aloft!" Turning his eyes from the scene below the boy gazed upward. He saw the blue sky, the fleecy clouds passing peacefully along, looking just the same as they did when he had looked at them while lying on his back on the green grass of the meadows in his country home. A strange feeling of peace and content came over him, and the feeling of dread, terror and despair passed away. His strength and presence of mind came back to him, and soon he was able to slide down the mast until he grasped a friendly rope, thence to the lower rigging, and on until the deck was again reached.

He never forgot the old sailor's advice given in the hour of need, and when he would feel dazed and fearful of danger, he would invariably look aloft until he recovered his mental balance.

We may well take a leaf from the old sailor's note-book, and impress his wisdom upon our minds. There's nothing so good in hours of trial, doubt, sorrow and pain, as to "look aloft." When we feel that we cannot see clearly with our spiritual vision—that our spiritual sight is blurred and dim—that we lose faith and confidence, hope and courage—that we feel the deadly sensation of despair and hopelessness creeping over us and benumbing our senses, stilling our heart—then is the time for us to listen to the warning shout: "Look aloft, lad; look aloft!"

When all seems lost—when darkness is closing around us—when we seem to have lost our foothold and have no way of regaining it—when all appears hopeless, gloomy and dreadful—when faith seems to have deserted us, and the chill of unbelief is on us—then is the time for us to shout to ourselves, "Look aloft—look aloft!"

When we try to solve the riddle of the universe—the problem of existence—by the aid of the intellect, unsupported by faith. When we ask our intellects, "Whence come I? Whither go I? What is the object of my existence? What does Life mean?" When we travel round and round the weary path of intellectual reasoning, and find that it has no ending. When we shout aloud the question of Life, and hear no answer but the despairing echo of our own sad cry. When Life seems a mockery—when Life seems to be without reason—when Life seems a torment devised by a fiend—when we lose the feeling of nearness to the Infinite Power that has supported us in the past—when we lose the touch of the Unseen Hand. These are the times for us to look upward to the source of Wisdom and Light. These are the times for us to heed the cry of the Soul: "Look aloft; look aloft; look aloft!"

Some clear night, when the moon is not shining, go out into the darkness, and gaze upward at the stars. You will see countless bright spots, each of which is a sun equaling or exceeding in size the sun which gives light and life to our little earth—each sun having its circling worlds, many of the worlds having moons revolving around them, in turn. Look all over the heavens, as far as the eye can reach, and endeavor to grasp the idea of the countless suns and worlds. Then try to imagine that in space, far beyond the reach of human vision, even aided by the telescope, are millions upon millions of other worlds and suns—on all sides of us, on and on and on throughout the Universe, reaching into Infinity. And then remember that all these worlds hold their places and revolve according to Law. And then remember that the microscope shows that Law manifests itself in the smallest thing that can be seen by its use. All around you you will see nothing but the manifestations of Law. And then, remembering that the Infinite, which has us all in charge, takes note of the fall of the sparrow, what has become of your fears and doubts and worries? Gone is your despair and unbelief, and in their place is found a reverent feeling of calm, peaceful Faith.

Aye, there is much good sense in the old sailor's maxim. "When you get rattled, LOOK ALOFT!"

To-Morrow

The work and cares of to-day easy if we do not worry about those of To-morrow—The mysterious To-morrow and its terrors—The way to meet the cares of To-morrow—To-morrow's opportunities will come as surely as To-morrow's cares—Law supreme—No need to be afraid—The real To-morrow.

The work of each day would be a pleasure if we would refrain from attempting to perform at the same time the work of to-morrow. The cares of to-day would cease to disturb us, if we would refuse to anticipate the cares of to-morrow. The work of to-day is easily performed, notwithstanding the fact that we spoiled the pleasure of yesterday by fretting about the tasks of the coming day. The cares of to-day do not seem half so terrible as they appeared viewed from the distance of yesterday, nor do we suffer nearly as much from to-day's burdens as we did yesterday in bearing these burdens in anticipation.

To-day is comparatively easy for us, but Oh, to-morrow. Aye, there's the trouble—to-morrow. The past is gone, and its sorrows, cares, troubles, misfortunes and work do not seem so terrible viewed from this distance—the misfortunes of the past are now often known as blessings in disguise. To-day is here, and we seem to be getting along fairly well—excepting fearing the dawn of to-morrow. But to-morrow—Oh! mysterious to-morrow—that delight of the child—that bugaboo of the "grown up"—what shall we say of to-morrow? Who knows what terrible monsters are lurking in its gloomy recesses—what frightful cares are slumbering there—what dreadful shapes are there crouching, with glowering eyes, awaiting our coming? No frightful tale of childhood begins to compare in horror with this fantasy of maturity—to-morrow.

Yesterday, with all its troubles—to-day, with its pressing tasks—affright us not, but to-morrow, ah! to-morrow. Tell us of the morrow! Who knows what a day may bring forth? Tell us how to meet the terrors of to-morrow! Forsooth, an easy task, good friends. The way to meet the terrors of to-morrow is to—wait until to-morrow.

The cares of to-morrow indeed! 'Twould be laughable if it were not so pitiful. To-morrow's cares may come, will come, must come, but what of to-morrow's opportunities, to-morrow's strength, to-morrow's chances, circumstances, helpers? Don't you know that the supply of good things does not cease with the close of to-day? Don't you know that in the womb of the future sleep opportunities intended for your use when the time comes? Don't you know that an earnest, confident expectation of the good things to come will cause these good things to grow for your use in the future? Well, it's so; they'll grow and grow and grow, and then when you need them you will find them ripe and ready to pick. Water them with Faith; surround them with the rich soil of Hope; let them receive the full rays of the sun of Love, and the nourishing fruit of Opportunity will be your reward—to-morrow.

Did you ever shiver with dread at the thought of what would happen if the sun should not rise to-morrow? Did you ever doubt that the grass would grow and the trees take on leaves next Spring? Did you ever fear that perhaps the Summer would not come? Oh, no, of course not! These things have always happened and you have sufficient faith to know that they will occur again. Yes, but you have been fearing that opportunities, chances, circumstances, may not be present to-morrow. Oh, ye of little faith do you not know that this is no world of chance? Do you not know that you are working under the operations of a great Law, and that these things are as much amenable to that Law as are the seasons, the crops, the motion of the earth, the planets, this and countless other solar systems, the UNIVERSE!

The Law which regulates the motions of the millions of worlds, and whose jurisdiction extends over Space—that Space the abstract idea of which cannot be grasped by the puny intellect of man of to-day—also takes cognizance of the tiny living organism too small to be seen through our strongest microscope. The sparrow's fall comes under the Law as well as the building of a magnificent series of solar systems. And yet, man fears to-morrow.

Of all living beings, man alone fears to-morrow. Children, lovers and philosophers escape the curse. The first two look forward to it with joy and confidence, having the love that casteth out fear; the philosopher's reason teaches him that which the intuition of the other two has grasped. The child intuitively recognizes that the infinite supply is inexhaustible and naturally expects to-morrow's supply as he does to-morrow's sun. He has faith in the Law, until Fear is suggested into his receptive mind by those who have grown old enough to fear. The child knows that "there are just as good fish in the sea as ever were caught," but the "grown-up" fears that to-day's fish is the last in the sea, and fails to appreciate to-day's haul by reason of his worry about the possible future failure of the fishing industry.

Oh No! I do not believe in just sitting down and folding my hands and waiting for "mine own to come to me." I know that "mine own will come to me," because I am doing well the work that the Law has placed before me to do—that which lies nearest to my hand to-day. I believe in work, good work, honest work, cheerful work, hopeful work, confident work. I believe in the joy of work—the pleasure of creating. And I believe that he who does his best work one day at a time working with faith, hope and confidence in the morrow, with Fear eliminated from his mind and replaced with Courage—I believe, I say, that such a man will never find his cupboard empty, nor will his children want for bread.

And furthermore, I believe that to-morrow is what we make it by our thoughts to-day. I believe that we are sowing thought-seeds to-day, which will grow up over night and bear fruit to-morrow. I believe that "Thought takes form in Action," and that we are, and will be, just what we think ourselves into being. I believe that our minds and bodies are constantly being molded by our thoughts, and that the measure of man's success is determined by the character of his thoughts. And I believe that when man will throw off the incubus of Fear, the frightful vision of the night will vanish, and, opening his eyes, in the place of the monster he will see the fair form and smiling face of a radiant creature, who, bending over him with love-lit eyes, will softly whisper, "I am TO-MORROW."

In The Depths of The Soul

Stores of information; rich mines of knowledge; uncut gems and precious metal awaiting the discoverer—Psychic and spiritual faculties—Strange attraction of soul to soul—The Rock of Ages—The Voice of the Soul.

Deep down in the soul are stores of information awaiting to be brought to the surface of consciousness. Rich mines of knowledge are there—uncut gems rest there awaiting the day when they will be uncovered and brought into the bright light of consciousness—rich veins of precious metals are there awaiting in patience the day when some Divine Adventurer will search for them and bring them to light. The human mind is a wonderful storehouse, concealing all sorts of treasures and precious things, only a fraction of which have been discovered so far.

We have faculties not yet recognized by the science of the day—psychic and spiritual faculties—just as real as the recognized faculties, playing an important part in our everyday lives, particularly when we have been made aware of their existence. In many of us these faculties are scarcely recognized, and many of us doubt and deny their very existence. Others have a faint perception of their existence, but do not know how to use them, and get but the slightest benefit from them. Others have awakened to the wonderful faculties which are developing and unfolding within them, and a few have gone so far as to aid in this development of these higher faculties of the mind, and have been almost startled at the results obtained. The Orientals have their ways of development of these faculties, and we Occidentals have ours. Each best serves the purposes of the particular people using it.

As we bring these faculties out of the realm of the super-conscious into the field of consciousness, life takes on an entirely different meaning, and many things heretofore dark are seen plainly and understood. No one can understand the Oneness of things until his spiritual faculties are sufficiently developed to make him *conscious* of it. Blind belief or reliance upon the words of another will never do for the seeker after Truth that which is accomplished by a single gleam of consciousness resting upon some of the hidden treasures of the soul. One glimpse into the depths of the soul will do more than the reading of thousands of books, the teaching of hundreds of teachers. This glimpse, once had, will never be forgotten. Its reality may be questioned at times—at other times the memory may seem dim and unreliable—but it will return in all its freshness and brightness, and even in the moment of doubt we cannot entirely escape it.

Our real knowledge of the existence of GOD is not obtained from the intellect. We can take up the subject of GOD and reason about it all our life, only to find ourselves, in the end, in a worse muddle than when we started. And yet one single ray of consciousness reaching down into the depths of our inner being will bring to us such a complete certainty of GOD'S existence and being, that nothing afterward will ever shake our faith in the reality and existence of the Supreme Power. We will not understand the nature of his being—his existence—his power—but we will *know* that he exists, and will feel that peacefulness and infinite trust in him which always come with the glimpse of the Truth. We will not understand any better the many theories of Man regarding GOD and his works; in fact, we will be more apt to turn away, wearied, from Man's discussion of the subject—the attempt of the finite to describe and limit the infinite. But we will *know* that at the Center of things is to be found that Universal Presence, and we feel that we can safely rest ourselves on his bosom—trust ourselves in his hands. The cares, sorrows and trials of Life seem very small indeed when viewed from the absolute position, although from the relative position this world often seems to be a very hell.

Another glimpse into the recesses of the soul reveals to us the Oneness of things. We see GOD as the great Center of things, and all the Universe as but One. The Oneness of all Life becomes apparent to us and we feel in touch not only with all mankind, but with all life. The petty distinctions of class, race, rank, caste, nationality, language, country fade away and we see all men as brothers. And we feel a kindly feeling and love toward the lesser manifestations of life. Even the rocks and the stones are seen as parts of the Whole and we no longer feel a sense of separateness from any thing. We realize what the Universe is, and in our imagination visit the most distant stars and instinctively know that we would find nothing foreign to us there—all would be but bits of the same thing.

And we begin to understand those strange attractions of soul to soul, instances of which have come to all of us. We realize that it is possible to entertain a feeling of love for every living creature—to every man or woman, the manifestations, of course, varying in degree and kind, according to sex and closeness of soul relation. It makes us more tolerant and causes us to see but ignorance in many things in which we saw but sin before. It makes us feel pity rather than hate. Ah, these little glimpses into the inmost recesses of the soul they teach us many new lessons.

And one of the greatest lessons that we may acquire in this way is the recognition of the eternal life of the soul. We may believe, with greater or less earnestness, in the doctrine of the immortality of the soul, our beliefs and conceptions depending more or less upon the teachings which we have received from early childhood, but until we become conscious of that which lies within us, we are never really certain—we do not know. Many good people will deny this statement, and will say that they have never doubted the life of the soul after death, but see how they act. When death comes into their houses they mourn and cry aloud in their agony, and demand of GOD why he has done this thing. They drape themselves in mourning and mourn and weep as if the loved one had been destroyed and annihilated. All of their actions and conduct go to prove that they have no abiding sense of the reality of the continuance of life beyond the grave. They speak of the dead as if they were lost forever—as if a sponge had been passed over the slate of life and naught remained. How cold and hollow sounds the would-be comforting words of friends and relatives, who assure the mourning ones that the being who has just laid aside the body is "better off now," and that all is "for the best," and all the rest of conventional expressions that we make use of. I tell you that one who has had a glimpse into what lies within him knows so well that he is eternal that he finds it impossible to look upon death in the ordinary way, and if he is not very careful he will be regarded as heartless and unfeeling for the sorrows of others. And he will be regarded as a fool in his views of life by those around him who attend church regularly every Sunday, and who profess a full belief in all its doctrines. If he considers that he himself is his soul, and that he is as much an immortal being now as he ever will be—that his body is but as a garment to cover him, or an instrument through which he manifests himself—if he considers that he is in eternity now just as much as he ever will be; that he cannot be destroyed by Mt. Pelee eruptions or railroad accidents—if, in short, he feels these things so strongly that they have become a part of his real everyday life—why, he is looked upon as "queer" by those who hear these things taught them every Sunday, and who would feel horrified if they were accused of harboring a doubt regarding them. This is one of the things that go to show the difference between "believing" a thing and "being conscious" of it.

Now, don't run away and say that I held that the church-goers have no conception of the reality of the immortality of the soul, for I haven't said any such thing. There are many church-goers who have experienced a full realization of the feeling I mention, and there are many more church-goers who have not. And there are many men and women who scarcely ever enter within the walls of a church who have had this experience, and it means more to them than all the preachments they have ever listened to. It is not a matter of being "in-church" or "out-of-church," it is a matter of spiritual development, that's all. I attend churches of all denominations, and I find all of them good. The service of the Catholic Church appeals to me, and so does the meeting of some old-fashioned Methodist congregation. I do not accept all the doctrines and theories I hear in the various churches, but I manage to get some good out of all. If I have any preference whatever, it is for an old-fashioned Quaker meeting, where, perhaps, not a word is said from beginning to close, but where there is undoubtedly a strong spiritual power manifested. I have even found much good in attending a certain orthodox church, where the venerable preacher, who does not believe in the "higher criticism" or creed revision, often gives us a delightful sermon on the horrors of hell and the state of the damned, including the unbaptized infants. I can listen to a sermon like this with a thrill of delight—a feeling of intense joy which comes to me because I have been given the inward assurance that there exists a GOD who is Love, instead of the hating, wrathful, vengeful creature that the poor preacher tries to make us believe is the Infinite Power—the Universal Presence—the Loving Father. Oh, no, I am not condemning churches—I like them all, and think that each one is doing the best possible work for the particular people who are attracted to it. I have listened to the exercises of the Salvation Army, and have seen much good in it. How many of you New Thought people, or you high-toned church members, would make half the sacrifices for what you consider Truth that the Salvation Army soldier or the Hallelujah lassie make every day of their lives? Stop a moment before you laugh at them. Some of these people have more spirituality in their little finger than many of us have in our whole bodies.

There are times when we feel disturbed and full of unrest. We seek to use our intellects and solve all the problems of life. We fret and chafe under the restrictions which have been placed upon us. We wish to KNOW all things. We reason this way and that way, follow up every lane, alley and street in the city of Thought, but, alas, we find not that which we seek. And in our search we are apt to forget that we have within us an assurance that all is well with the world, and with us. We rebel against the leadings of the Spirit—against the knowledge that has come from the inner self—and we want to get our knowledge over the old channels—by means of the Intellect. Well, at such times we storm and fume and fret, and complain at our inability to solve the problem. We set up ideas only to tear them down again. We assume and then abandon one position after another, until there is nothing left. And the end of all the intellectual debauch is to say finally, "I do not know." And then, after the struggle is over, we see, just as plainly as ever before, the glimpse of Truth that has come to us from within—we hear the words of the soul—we have the same old consciousness. We say to ourselves, "I may not get this thing intellectually, but I KNOW it is true. I cannot doubt the voice of the Soul."

This knowledge which comes from within is like the rock against which beat the storms of the sea—against which dash the waves which completely cover it and which hide it from sight, until it seems that it has disappeared forever from view, carried away by the attacking waves. The lightning flashes, the thunder rolls, the fury of the tempest seems concentrated against this rock, and the demon of the storm seems intent upon destroying every particle of it—of tearing it to little bits with which to strew the shores. All is darkness—all is blackness—all is fury, raging and terror. After hours, the storm subsides, and then later morning comes, and the first rays of the rising sun kiss lovingly the rock which has stood the fury of the storm, and has emerged unhurt, a witness to its superiority to the elements.

Storm away, ye who would destroy this rock—dash your waves of Doubt, Logic, Criticism, Unbelief, Dogma, Theory, against this rock of the Spirit. Exert yourself to the utmost—expend all the force that is within you—do your best—do your worst. Tear and twist, pull and wrench, beat and pound, and what have you accomplished? After the storm has passed away—after the clouds have dispersed—when the sky again is blue and the sun again is shining—the rock still stands, undisturbed, unchanged, unshaken. And stand it will for ages and ages. And Man shall begin to know of the stability and firmness of this rock. He will begin to realize just what it means to him, and he will know that while the waves that beat upon it are good and needful, and not to be despised, that only upon the rock can he safely build.

Do not despise the intellect and its teachings, but know that ye have within ye another source of knowledge—that ye have spiritual faculties which are developing and which you can use. And trust the work of these faculties—listen to the voice of the Soul.

"Forget It"

Why worry about the past?—Hugging old sorrows to your bosom—What to do with them—Don't poison your life—Pain brings experience—Learning your lesson—How to get rid of a gloomy thought—Throw it away—Forget it.

One can often get some useful lesson from the slang and current phrases of the day. There is something particularly attractive to me about slang, and the pat phrases that are passed along from one to another on the streets. Many of these phrases condense in a few words certain practical truths that one could use as a basis for a sermon, an essay, or even a book. They are the practical experiences of the people crystallized in a catchy phrase. The phrase which I hear so frequently on the street just now, "Forget it," seems to me to contain much practical common sense, and if people would put it into practice there would be many more brighter faces—many more lighter hearts. What's the use, anyhow, of carrying around a long face or a heavy heart, just because away back in the past something "went wrong" with us, or even if we "went wrong" ourselves (and most of us have—I have, I know)? What's the use? Forget it!

Of course you will not forget the experiences of the past, and you do not want to. That's one of the things we are living for—gaining experience. When we have once really learned a thing through experience, we never forget it—it is a part of us. But why bother about the memory of the pain, the mortification, the "slip-up," the heartache, the wounded feelings, the misplaced confidence, the thing done in the wrong way, the chance you let slip by, the folly, the sin, the misery, the "might-have-beens," and all the rest. Oh what's the use? Forget it I say, forget it.

If one is to worry about all the things that went wrong—all the things that didn't come right—in the past; if he has to take out each memory every day, and after carefully dusting it off, fondle and caress it, and hug it close to his bosom; if he has to raise up these ghosts from the past—these phantoms of long ago—these musty, moth-eaten things—why he will have no time for the affairs of to-day. He will lose all the joy of the now—all the pleasure of life of the moment—all the interest in the things of to-day. Oh, dear, dear, what's the use? Forget it—forget it.

Some people are not happy unless they have some old faded sorrow hugged up close to their bosoms, and they feel guilty if they happen to smile and forget the old thing for even a moment. Oh, how they do gloat over their own revamped unhappiness—how they enjoy the relieving of the pains and sorrows, mistakes and ignorance of years gone by. How they love to hold the fox to their sides and let it eat out their heart. These people are really happy in the unhappiness, and life would not be worth living if they were deprived of their pet sorrows. Of course, if these people are really happy because they are unhappy, I have no objection. Every man or woman has the right to pursue happiness in his or her own way, and I suppose that that is as good a way as any other, and I should not find fault if somebody else's way is different from mine. But doesn't it seem like a pity to see people wasting their time, energy, thoughts and life on these old sorrows? If they must think of the past, why not think of the bright things that came into their lives, instead of the dark ones? Think of the moments of happiness, not of the moments of sorrow. Don't make a tomb of your mind. Don't let that particular painful experience poison your present life. Don't do it—don't do it. What's the use? Forget it.

Every bit of pain that has happened you has brought its experience to you—you are better, wiser and broader for it. Look at it in that way, and you will cease to mourn and wail and wring your hands over the fact that in the past you "have done those things which you ought not to have done, and have left undone those things which you ought to have done." Nonsense! You have gained the experience and know better now. If you were placed back in the same old position, and lacked the experience that you have gained by just such things, you would do the same old thing over again, and in the same old way. You couldn't help it, because you would be the same old person. What you would like to do would be to be placed back in the same position, and face the same old temptation or problem, but you would want to take with you the experience you have gained by your former mistake. You want the cake and the penny at the same time. You want the experience without the pain. Oh, yes, you do, now, that's just what you want—I've been through it myself, and know all about it. You've gained the experience, be satisfied. Some day you'll need that experience, and will be glad you have it, and will see that it was worth all you've paid for it. No, you don't see it that way? Well, maybe you haven't had enough of it—haven't learned your lesson yet. If that is the case, some of these days the law will drop you back into the pot, until you're well done. The law is not satisfied with underdone people. Oh, you're making a big mistake. Forget it—forget it.

The people who carry these old things around with them generally get themselves into the mental attitude that draws other things of the same sort to them. Misery likes company, and a miserable thought also likes companionship, and almost always manages to attract some other miserable thing to it, to keep it from being lonesome. The only way to get rid of a thought of this kind is to—forget it.

Now if you have some pet thing that is gnawing out your vitals—is corroding your heart—is poisoning your mind—take it out and look at it for the last time. Give it a last long lingering gaze. Kiss it good-bye. Weep over it if you like, for this is the last you will see of it. Then throw open the window of your mind and pitch it out into the outer darkness.

FORGET IT!

"The Kindergarten of God"

Life a great school—Man a child learning his lesson—Preparing for higher grades—The game-task—What it all means—Things as they are—The rules wise and good—Each task means something—Greeting the Kindergartner.

I see Life as a great school—Man as a tiny child, learning his little lessons, performing his little tasks, playing his little games, enjoying his little pleasures, suffering his little pains, disappointments, trials and sorrows.

I feel that we are in but the kindergarten stage of existence, learning the first lessons of Life—fitting ourselves for the grander, broader, fuller life in store for us. And I feel that this little kindergarten experience will continue until we have learned its lessons well—have firmly grasped the principles designed for our baby minds. And I feel that when we have proven our ability to weave our little mats—build our little blocks—draw our little pictures—mold our little clay forms—sing our little songs—then, and not until then, will we pass into a higher grade, where we will spell out the lines of the Primer of Life, and acquire the elementary principles of Cosmic Mathematics. And I feel that each little lesson must be learned, thoroughly, before the next step is taken. And I feel that every one of us must perform his own task—must memorize his own lesson—before he can gain the experience—can profit by the knowledge acquired in the performance of the task. We may be inspired by some brighter pupil—be encouraged by the loving sympathy of some fellow-scholar, but the task is *ours* to perform, sooner or later—and ours is the joy of accomplishment.

I believe that as some children, even whilst fascinated by the game-task of the kindergarten, know that it is only a childish task and not the *real thing* of life, so may we come to a point, where, whilst enjoying the constantly changing play of life, we will realize that it is but the training for greater things, and important only in that sense. The perception of this fact by the child need not interfere with his interest in the game—need not prevent him from feeling the joy of *doing*, creating, working, gaining new experiences; nor need it prevent *us* from playing the kindergarten games of grown-up life with a zest and interest, not alone because we realize that we are learning valuable lessons, but, yea, even from the very excitement and joy of the game itself.

When we realize just what this view of Life means, we will find new pleasures in everyday life—will learn to laugh with childish glee at our little successes in molding the clay into the desired shape—in the clever weaving of the mat. And we will learn to smile, through our tears, if our little mat happens to tear in two—if our little clay sphere drops to the floor and is shattered—if the hour's work is destroyed.

And we will learn our little lesson of Love—of Comradeship. We will learn by experience that if we lead the narrow, selfish life we will miss the joy that falls to the lot of those who have learned to express more fully the love-nature within them—we will find that Love begets Love—that the love-nature, expressed, attracts to itself the love in the hearts of our little playmates. We will find that the child who carries within him the love for others, and expresses that love, need never want for friends or companions, need never suffer from loneliness, need never fear being left out in the cold. The true Personal Magnetism of the child (and the grown-up) consists largely of—Love, which never fails in its drawing power. And we will learn, from bitter experience, the folly of the idea of separateness from our little playmates—will know that the standing apart brings nothing but sorrow to us. We will realize that selfishness brings nothing but pain—that giving has its pleasures as well as receiving. And we will learn something of Brotherhood, and its goodness—we will have the True Democracy of the kindergarten impressed upon us. These lessons (and others) we will learn well, before passing on.

We, like the child, often wonder what is the use of it all—fret over our enforced tasks—chafe at the confinement—rage at the restrictions, and, failing to comprehend it all, indulge in complaints, protests, rebellion. And, like the child, we cannot expect to understand the whyness of it all, certainly not until we pass beyond the kindergarten stage of existence and reach the higher grades.

When one begins to realize *what he is*—begins to be conscious of the I AM—begins to know things as they are—he gradually learns to appreciate things at their true worth, and, although not released from the necessity of playing out his kindergarten game tasks, is able to, practically, *stand aside and watch himself play them out*. He knows that he is gaining knowledge—is mastering his lessons—is living-out, and out-living, his desires—is acquiring and storing up new experiences—but he values things only at their final worth, and is not deceived by the apparent value of the moment. He begins to see things in their proper relations. He does not take himself (or things) too seriously. He enjoys the pleasure of the game—but he knows it to be but the play and pleasure of the child—he laughs, but is not deceived. He suffers, also, the sorrow, grief, disappointment, humiliation and chagrin of the child-nature—but even though the tears are falling he, *knowing*, smiles. He laughs with joy—with pain he cries, but he knows—he *knows*. He enjoys the playthings, gifts, rewards, but he knows them for what they are—he knows. He plays the games with the children who do not know—and well he plays—but he knows. His disillusionment spoils not the sport—he plays on (for play he *must*), knowing, but enjoying. Yes, enjoying *because* of the knowing. He knows that the child-things are good—but he sees them as but shadows of the Good to come. He knows that he "cannot escape from his own good." And he knows that the Good is also in store for his playmates (though they know it not) and, being full of love, he rejoices.

He feels that the rules of the School are wise and good, and that, though he cannot see it clearly now, INFINITE JUSTICE rules all, as will in the end appear. He knows that promotion will be gained, just as soon as earned. He knows that just as soon as he is able to master a task, that task will be set before him—not a moment before. And he knows that no task will be allotted him even one moment before the possibility of its accomplishment.

He knows that he is being tested, trained and strengthened, day by day—that every unpleasant and disagreeable task has an important end in view. And he knows that every task placed before him is in accordance with a Law that takes cognizance of his powers, failings, capabilities, short-comings—that understands him better than he does himself. He knows that the very allotment of the task is a guarantee of his ability to perform it. He knows that within him are latent powers, potential forces, hidden knowledge, which will well forth from his sub-conscious mentality when bidden by the Confident Expectation of Intelligent Faith.

And, knowing these things, he is filled with Courage—and presses forth eagerly to the tasks of the day. And, knowing, he casts off all Fear, Worry, Discouragement and Discontent, and, with the smile of Love on his face and the joy of Faith in his heart, he greets THE KINDERGARTNER with Confidence and Trust.

The Human Wet Blanket

Sees no good in anything—Expects the bad and gets it—Attracts it to him—Depresses everything and everyone—Carries an aura of negative depressing thought—Clammy—Puts out the fire of energy—Take warning.

Did you ever meet the Human Wet Blanket?

To start with, he sees no good in anything. To him every man is a rogue—every woman a schemer trying to pull the wool over the eyes of some man. He looks for the Bad—expects to find it—and find it he does. One generally gets what he looks for. He attracts to him that for which he looks, and he cannot see any other qualities than those possessed by himself. Everyone is trying to cheat him, and out-wit him, so he thinks, and I have no doubt that the Law brings him a fair share of people of this kind. In order to prevent other people from taking advantage of him, he endeavors to take advantage of them in the same small way that he fears they will use on him. The consequence is the people with whom he has dealings are apt to give him a dose of his own medicine. He trusts no man. He's so shrewd that he measures off a spool of thread in order to be sure that the storekeeper has not robbed him of a yard or two. And the funny thing is, that he sets in motion the Law which causes the one short-measure spool in the case to fall into his hands. He just *draws* these things to him. He thinks himself a marvel of cunning, and endeavors to manifest it in petty practices, the result being that he attracts to himself all the little schemers, and some of the big ones, who happen to be within the radius of his attracting power, while the other type of people are repelled by his mental attitude and thought-force. Funny, isn't it?

Then he sees nothing but disaster ahead in any plan, and, sure, enough, if he gets near enough to the plan to contaminate it, trouble is sure to happen. As an attractor of Negative Thought he is a glittering success. He seems to have a positive genius for doing things the wrong way. And yet, he doesn't believe in the Attractive Power of Thought or "any such nonsense."

He's too shrewd to take any stock in such ridiculous theories, although he exhibits in his life a most convincing proof of the truth of New Thought teachings.

He never says "I Can and I Will," and if he hears anyone around him indulging in such heretical notions, he promptly proceeds to squelch him by a few "Supposings," "Buts," "What ifs," and two or three gloomy shakes of the head, and a few sighs. His motto seems to be "There's no use trying, you can't do it." With him the country seems always to be going to the dogs, and the poorhouse is constantly looming up before him.

I need scarcely add that Fear, Worry, Jealousy, and Suspicion are his bosom friends. He holds these thoughts constantly, and they and the rest of the negative brood are devouring him. They are making their home in his mentality and are increasing rapidly, besides frequently inviting their friends for a visit.

Of course, it's nobody's business if he likes this sort of thing, but it is not pleasant to come in contact with him. He is surrounded with an aura of negative, depressing, gloomy, thought-force, which is manifest to all with whom he comes in contact. Turn him loose in a roomful of cheerful people, and in a few minutes the conversation has lagged, the warmth of love and friendship has disappeared and things begin to feel damp and chilly, and someone will begin to make inquiry regarding the furnace or the steam radiators, and wondering why the janitor does not keep up the fire on such a day. Approach him when you feel fired with energy, ambition and push—when you feel that you can go out and conquer any obstacle—and you will feel the clammy wet blanket thrown over you, putting out your fire of energy, and in a moment or two you will wonder "What's the use." That is, unless you understand your business, and know how to throw off the influence of the negative thought-waves emanating from this man. Look out for him.

From the bottom of my heart, I pity this man and his kind. He gets none of the sweet things of Life—he doesn't see them lying around. He misses the joy of living. He sees everything through jaundiced eyes. He knows nothing of the happiness of the clear head, warm heart, and brotherly hand. He is so occupied in looking for the spoiled fruit on the ground that he does not see the perfect fruit on the branches above his head, begging to be picked. He is so much engrossed in the mud upon the road, that he does not see the bright blue sky above his head; the beautiful landscape; the children playing on the grass; the mother nursing her babe; the old couple trudging along hand in hand. These things do not exist for him. His mind is so full of Fear, Suspicion, Distrust, and Petty Spite, that Love finds no room. But even this is Good—for many find their way to Optimism only by first sinking to the depths of extreme Pessimism. They reach the Celestial City by the road that winds through the Valley of the Shadow of Death. Even these things shall pass away.

All's well.

Aim Straight

Fear attracts, as well as Desire—Learn to aim straight and aim at the right thing—Examples—The bowler—The bicyclist and the car—The bicyclist and the post—The boy and the marbles—Wisdom from the babe—Look straight; Think straight; Shoot straight.

A strong Desire or a strong Fearthought is an aim at the thing desired or feared. And in proportion to the degree of Desire or Fear, will we be carried toward the thing at which we aim. Confident Expectation is manifested in a Fearthought as well as in an earnest Desire, and when we confidently expect a thing to happen we are carried toward it by an irresistible force. It may seem strange to you to hear that Fear is akin to Desire, but this is the truth. It matters not whether we call it Desire or Fear, the gist of the matter lies in the Confident Expectation. A faint Hope and a lurking Fear have about the same attractive force—a Desire coupled with a firm belief in its realization attracts strongly, but no more strongly than does a Fear coupled with a feeling of certainty of its realization. The thing upon which your Thought is firmly fixed or drawn toward, will be the thing you will realize. Therefore Aim Straight.

We have heard much of the Attractive Power of Thought as applied to Desire. I will now say something to you about the same force called into operation by Fearthought. It is far more pleasant for me to speak of the bright side of the question, but I would be neglecting my duty toward you if I failed to direct your attention to the reverse of the shield. When you thoroughly realize that Thought-force works both ways, you will know how to handle it, and will understand many things that have heretofore been dark to you. You will learn to AIM STRAIGHT, but will also learn to be careful at what you aim. You will learn to avoid the aim inspired by Fear, and will hereafter use all your energies to pointing your mental arrow at the bull's-eye of Happiness and Success.

Let us take a few facts from the physical plane in order to illustrate things as they are on the mental plane of effort. Life has its correspondences on all its planes, and by taking examples from one plane, we will be able to more readily understand the workings of the Law on other planes.

Some time ago, I was talking to a number of people about this subject, and gleaned from each an illustration of the workings of the Law of Attraction on the physical plane. And each example although on the physical plane, showed the power of Mind behind it. I will tell you what some of these people said, and you can see for yourself just what I mean.

The first man was a printer, who after hours spent much time in bowling, and who was looked upon as an expert in that game. He said that some time before he was playing a game, and at a critical point when he was taking aim and endeavoring to put the ball in between the 1 and 2 pins (a specially advantageous shot), his opponent spoke up and said "Just watch him hit the 4 pin." I do not know anything about bowling, but it seems that to hit the 4 pin is about the worst thing that can happen to a bowler, outside of missing the pins altogether. Well, to go on with the story, with the remark of his rival, Fearthought entered the mind of the printer, and he couldn't get the 4 pin out of his mind. He kept on looking at the place he wanted to hit, but his mind was on the 4 pin, and he feared that he would hit it. To use his own words, he "got rattled," and away went the ball striking the 4 pin fair and square. He concluded the story by saying: "And so instead of making a 'ten strike' I got only a 'split.'" Maybe you understand those terms better than do I, but at any rate you will see what a Fearthought brought to this typographical bowler in his little game of ten-pins. Moral: When you wish to place the ball Energy between the 1 and 2 pins of Life, don't allow Fearthoughts to switch you off to the 4 pin, thereby giving you a "split" instead of the coveted "ten-strike."

Another friend told me that, a few days before, he had been riding on the front bench of a grip-car on a Chicago cable-line. Hearing the gripman break into the vernacular in a vigorous style, he looked up, and saw a colored man on a bicycle trying to cross the track "on the bias," as the girls say, just ahead of the car. There was plenty of time—plenty of room—for the man to get across, but when he reached the middle of the track Fearthought got hold of him, and in spite of himself his wheel turned and he headed straight for the car. He headed straight for the gripcar, just as if he had aimed at it, and the next moment he went "bang" right into it. He escaped injury, but his wheel was wrecked. When asked about it, he said that from the moment he got afraid of the car his wheel "ran away with him," right into the thing he Feared. Moral: Keep your mind fixed on the thing you want—not on the thing you don't want.

Another man, to whom I related the story of the man on the wheel, said that he had the same trouble when he was learning to ride the wheel. He was getting along pretty well and could manage to steer half-way straight, although in a wobbly manner, until one day he happened to see a certain telegraph pole in front of the place where he was learning to ride. The pole seemed to hypnotize him, and from that day he couldn't keep his front wheel away from it. He couldn't keep away from that pole—he was afraid of it. The pole seemed to have magnetic qualities and the result was "Bump." He remounted, over and over again, but the result was the same. At last he made up his mind that he was going to get ahead of that pole somehow, and he mounted the wheel with his back toward the pole (but his Mind was still on it) and lo! the front wheel described a semi-circle, and back to the pole he went. Moral: Don't let a pole hypnotize you with Fearthought—keep your Mind on the place to which you wish to go.

But the best example was given by a boy who had kept his eyes open and his thinker working. Maybe I had better tell you in his own words. This is what he said, just as he said it:

"Oh, pshaw!" said the Boy, "you're making a big fuss over nothing. Every feller knows that you've got to *think* about a thing if you want to hit it, and if you think about the wrong thing, why, you'll hit the wrong thing. If I fire a stone at a tin can, why, I just look square at the can and think about the can for all I'm worth, and the can's a dead one, sure. If I happen to let my mind wander to the cat what's on the shed over to the left of the can—well, so much the worse for the cat, that's all. *To shoot straight, you've got to aim straight; and to aim straight you've got to look straight; and to look straight you've got to think straight.* Every kid knows that, or he couldn't even play marbles. If I get my heart set on a beauty marble in the ring, I just want it the worst way and says I to myself, 'You're my marble.' Then I look at him strong and steady-like and don't think about nothing else in the world but that beauty. Maybe I'm late for school, but I clean forget it. I don't see nothing—nor think nothing—but that there marble what I want. As the piece in my reader says, it's my 'Heart's Desire,' and I don't care whether school keeps or not, just so as I get it. Then I shoot, and the marble's mine. And, at school, when our drawing teacher tells us how to draw a straight line, she makes two dots, several inches away from each other. Then she makes us put our pencils on the first dot and look steady at the other and move our pencil towards it. The more you keep thinking about the far off dot, and the less you think about the starting dot or your hand, the straighter you're going to get your line. Wonst I looked straight at the far-off dot with my eyes, but I kept thinking about a red-headed girl on the other side of the room, and what do you think, the line I was drawing slanted away off in her direction, although I had kept my eyes glued on the far-away dot and never even peeped in the kid's direction. That shows, sure, that it's the thinking as well as the looking. See?"

All of the examples above given contain within them the principles of a mighty truth—a working illustration of a great law of Life. If we are wise we will profit by them. Many things are happening around us every day, from which we might gain lessons if we would only think a little, instead of playing "follow my leader" and accepting other people's thought, ready made. We have gotten so accustomed to these "hand-me-down" thoughts, that we have almost forgotten how to turn out thoughts for ourselves. The day has come when we are required to do a little thinking on our own account, instead of humbly bowing before moth-eaten Authority perched upon a crumbling base. The time has arrived when we must strike out for ourselves, instead of following a musty Precedent which has "seen better days." This is the age of the Individual. This the time for the "I" to assert itself.

I wish you would pay attention to what the Boy said. It is not the first time that we have gone to the babe for wisdom. Although a child has an imagination beyond our comprehension, he, at the same time, is painfully and even brutally, matter of fact. He is continually asking: "Why," and when we grown-ups are unable to answer him he answers the question himself, often better than we could have done. He doesn't theorize, but gets down to business, and works things out for himself. This boy knew all about the Thinking part of the problems, and had put it into practical application, while we were theorizing about it. He had discovered that in order to get things we must first earnestly Desire them; then Confidently Expect that we would get them; then go to work to procure them. That's the true philosophy of getting things. He tells us, about the marble, that he first "wanted it the worst way" and "didn't care whether school kept or not" just so he got the marble. Then he "looked strong and steady-like" at the marble, saying: "You're my marble." Then he shot, and the marble was his. Can any of you describe the process of getting things better than this? If we grown-ups would only put into our daily tasks the interest and attention that the boy put into his game of marbles, we would "get the marble" oftener than we have been doing.

Of course, it may be true, that the principal joy is in the getting of things rather than in the possession of them—that the Game of Life is like the game of marbles in that respect, but what of that? That needn't spoil the game. The boy knows enough to enjoy playing for a few marbles that may be obtained for a penny-a-fistful at the corner store—but that fact doesn't bother him at all. He knows that when he gets the marble it will not seem half so beautiful in the hand as it did in the ring—but he gets ready to shoot for the next one with just as much zest and enjoyment. He finds a joy in Living; Acting; Doing; Expressing; Growing and Outgrowing, Gaining Experiences. Take a lesson from the Boy—while you are in the Great Game, take a boy's interest in it; play with a zest; play your level best, and *get the marble*. The Boy instinctively knows that the joy of life consists of Living, while we poor grown-ups vainly imagine that our pleasure will come only in the trophies of the game—the glass-marbles of Life—and look upon the playing of the game as drudgery and work imposed upon us as a punishment of the sins of our forefathers. The boy lives in the Now, and enjoys every moment of his existence—his winnings, his losings, his victories, his defeats, while we, his elders and superiors in wisdom groan at the heat of the day and the rigor of the game and are only reconciled to our tasks by the thought of how we will enjoy the possession of the marbles, when we get them at the end of the game. The Boy sucks his orange and extracts every particle of its sweet contents, while we throw away the juicy meat and aim only to secure the pips. Oh, yes! the boy not only knows how to "get there," but he has also a sane philosophy of Life. Many of us grown-ups are now re-learning that which we lost with our youth.

You will notice that the bowler, the bicyclists and the others, got what they didn't want, because they were afraid of it, and allowed it to distract their thoughts from the object of their Desire. To Fear a thing is akin to Desiring it—in either case you are attracted toward it, or it to you. It's a rule that works both ways. You must think about the Thing you Want—not about the Thing you Don't Want, for the thoughts you are thinking are the ones that are going to take form in action, as the Boy said: "*You've got to think about a thing if you want to hit it, and if you think about the wrong thing, why, you're going to hit the wrong thing*." Watch your Ideal, not your Bugbear. Concentrate on your Ideal—fix your thought and gaze upon it, like the boy upon his marble—and don't allow Fearthought to sidetrack you. Select the thing you want to be, and then grow steadily into it. Pick out the thing you want, and then go straight and steadily to it. Replace your old whine: "I Fear," with the New Thought shout: "I Can, and I Will." Then you will experience an illustration of "Thought taking form in Action."

Look Straight; Think Straight; Shoot Straight; in these three things lie the secret of Success.

At Home

Don't be afraid—You are at home—Not here by chance—You belong here—YOU are the soul—YOU cannot be hurt—YOU cannot be banished—YOU are right in the universe, and there is no outside—Great things are before you—Make yourself at home.

Don't be afraid. You're living in your own home. This Universe was built for you to inhabit—to occupy—to enjoy. Do not feel strange—make yourself at home. The wonderful laws of nature—those which have been discovered, and those which remain to be discovered—are all laws for your use, when you grow large enough to understand how to make use of them.

Did you think you were here by chance, or that you were an alien? If so, learn better. You are to the manor born—you are the heir. Everything around the place is for your use, when you grow up. No one can dispossess you—no one can put you out. You are at home.

Do you long for another home? Do you fret and chafe at the trials and troubles of this world, and imagine that somewhere else things will be better? Well, they'll never be better for you until you have met and conquered the trials and troubles of this place. You are just where you belong. You are surrounded with just the things you need. You are getting just what you deserve. And until you learn the truth of this, you will have the same surroundings—the same environments. And then when you learn that the things around you are all right—that you are being treated justly—that you are getting just what you have attracted, and are attracting, to yourself—then you will be ready for the next step in the journey, and you will have new surroundings and new environments—new tasks—new lessons—new pleasures.

I hear some of you talking about Death. You seem to think that you will be another order of being as soon as you take your last breath upon earth. You talk about being a "spirit," bye-and-bye. Do I believe this? Of course, I believe it. I *know* it. But I also know something else, and that is that you are a spirit now, just as much as you will be in another world. Did you think that some wonderful essence was going to grow from you, and that that essence would be what you call a spirit? Nonsense! YOU are the spirit, and the not-you part which will be discarded never was you. The You which says I AM is the real thing—the real self—and the rest of you is but tools and instruments which YOU are using. Why can't you see this? You talk about "my soul," "my spirit," and so on. You make me tired. Why, the thing which is thinking and speaking—YOU—is the "soul" or "spirit" of which you are talking. You talk as if the physical part of you, which is changing continually, was you. You are like the boy with the old knife. He was continually having the knife repaired. He had had seven new blades and three new handles put on it, and yet it was the same old knife. Why, you could step right out of your body (and maybe you do, more than you have any idea of) and it would be the same old YOU. You could discard your body just as you do your clothes, and yet YOU would be the same individual. There is a wonderful difference between individuality and personality. One you cannot get rid of; the other may be changed.

What's the use in being afraid? Nobody can hurt the real YOU. You cannot be wiped out of existence. If a single spirit atom should be destroyed, the entire structure would smash up. You cannot be banished from the Universe, for there's nowhere else to put you. You cannot get outside of the Universe, for *there's no outside*. There's no place for you outside of everywhere.

And you talk about time and eternity. Why, you're in eternity right now. You are right in it this moment. It is always to-day—to-morrow never comes. And you are right at home in the Universe, and always will be. You are always there, for there's nowhere else to go.

So what's the use in being afraid? Who's going to hurt you? They can't kill YOU. They can't put you out of existence. They cannot expel you from the Universe. So what are they going to do about it anyhow? And, after all, who are "They?" You talk as if there were outside forces and influences antagonistic to you. Outside of what? No matter what beings of earth or air there may be, they are creatures like yourself. They are all a part of the Whole Thing—all made of the same material—all come from the hand of the same maker—you are all cut from the same piece of goods. The apparent differences are illusions—the difference and separateness is only relative, and not actual.

So, make yourself at home. Take a look around and see what a nice bit of the Universe you have to live in. Some of your family have been trying to occupy the whole house instead of only their share of it, but those things are gradually working out, and all will be better within a comparatively short time. This is going to be a better world to live in when men take time to think a little. And you'll be around to enjoy it when it comes—never fear. You cannot get away, even if you want to.

And, what's the use of waiting for to-morrow. There's lots of things in which you can find happiness to-day, if you will only stop worrying about to-morrow. The little child knows more about enjoying life than you do. The little child feels at home anywhere and starts in to enjoy it, and get the most out of it, until he grows old enough to be hypnotized by the race belief.

You are at home here. Just as much at home as is the fish in the sea—the bird in the air. Realize this, and make the most of it. Stop being afraid. Stop fretting. Stop worrying. Realize that yesterday, to-day, and to-morrow, you are here in the Universe. It's a good Universe, and it grows better as man grows in wisdom to take advantage of its goodness. And it is not yet "sun-up" here. Great things are before us. And you will see them and take part in them. Make yourself at home, for you're going to be around here for some time.

The Solitude of The Soul

Lorado Taft's group—Description—Each stands alone—Each is in touch with every other—Soul communion in silence—Silence is the sanctuary of the soul—The oneness of life and its apparent separateness—The message.

In one of the rooms of the Art Institute, in Chicago, stands a remarkable group, by Lorado Taft, the sculptor, entitled "The Solitude of the Soul." The average visitor stops a moment and passes on, commenting on the beauty of the figures composing this group. A few hurry past, afraid to look at the figures, for they are nude—as naked as the human soul before the gaze of its Creator. (Some people are afraid of things not hidden by draperies—even the naked Truth shocks them.) But the man or woman who thinks and understands—stops long before this group, conscious that it tells the tale of a mighty truth.

Around a large rock, stand four human figures—two men and two women. They are so placed that but one figure is in full sight from any given point of view, although the connection between any figure and the two on each side of it may be seen. It is necessary to walk completely around the group to see the idea of the sculptor—to read the story that he has written into the marble.

Each figure has an individuality. Each stands alone. And yet each is in touch with the one behind, and the one before. Each one is connected with all, yet each one stands alone. One figure extends a hand to her brother just ahead of her, and on her shoulder rests the tired head of the brother following her. Hand in hand, or head on shoulder stand they, each giving to the other that human touch and contact so dear to the soul craving that companionship of one who understands.

Each face shows sorrow, pain, and longing—that longing for that complete union of soul with soul—that longing that earth-life cannot satisfy. And each feels and knows that the other has the same longing. And each gives to the other that comforting touch that says "I know—I know." Each face shows a great human love mingled with its pain. Each face shows resignation mingled with its grief. It is the old story of human love and human limitations. It is also a story of deeper import—the story of the soul.

Every lip is closed. Each man and woman is silent. And yet each understands the other. Soul is communing with soul, in the Silence. And in the Silence alone can soul converse with soul. Words cheapen the communication of soul to soul. With those who understand us well, we can best commune in Silence. Hand in hand—cheek to cheek—sit those who love well. The tale of love is told and re-told without a word. Words serve their purpose in conveying the commonplaces of life, but seem strangely inadequate to express the deeper utterances of the soul. The tale of love—the story of sorrow—needs no words. The soul understands the message of the soul—mind flashes the message to mind—and all is known. The fondest memory of the one whom you loved and lost, is not of moments in which he spoke even the most endearing words. The memory most sacred to you is that of some great Silence lived out with the loved one—some moment in which each soul drew aside its veil and gazed with awe into the depths of the other soul. Silence is the sanctuary of the soul. Enter it only with due reverence. Uncover the head—tread softly.

Each figure stands alone, and yet in touch with all the rest. Each is apparently separate and yet each is but a part of the whole. Each feels the frightful solitude which comes to the soul when first it recognizes what it is. And yet, in that dreadful moment each knows itself to be in touch with all of life. Each feels that intense longing for a closer soul union—a reunion of the separated parts of the whole. And yet each realizes the impossibility of the consummation of that desire at this time—and they show their grief—they place the head upon the shoulder of the other—they clasp the hand of the other—they touch the flesh of the other—all as a symbol of the desire for the union of the soul.

This group is a symbol of the oneness of life and its apparent separateness. A picture of the in-touchness of each part of the whole, with every other part. A story of the pain of the soul in its awful solitude—of its impotent striving for at-one-ment. A representation of the communion of soul with soul, in the Silence. A tale of the comfort and joy in the presence of another human form. A message of The Brotherhood of Man. All this—and more—is in this group.

I wonder if the sculptor saw it all, or whether he chiseled better than he knew. Sometimes the Divine in man causes him to write better—paint better—cut better—than he realizes. Others see much more in his essays, stories, poems, paintings, statuary, than the maker knew was there. And the man himself, after years have past again views his work, and wonders at the new story he reads there. He feels dazed at having portrayed truths of which he dreamt not while he worked. There are within us unexplored depths, of the existence of which we do not dream. And from these depths, now and then, rise into our consciousness beautiful thoughts—beautiful images—which we reproduce on paper—canvas—marble. We do not understand these things, and we join with others in the feeling of wonder inspired by the sight of the reproduction of that which came from the depths of our mental being. And some, who have grown closer to the Real Self within them, see beauties in our work to which we are blind. Not until the scales fall from our eyes, do we realize the full meaning of our work.

Some call this Inspiration. But those who have pierced the veil know that it is inspiration from within, not from without. It is the voice of the Divine spark within man, whispering to the consciousness which is struggling to know better that Higher Self—a whisper of encouragement and good cheer—a portent of the future—a glimpse of the distant light—a bestowal of a few crumbs from the table of the Spirit.

I know not, I say, whether Lorado Taft knew what he chiseled. I know not whether he is a man of deep spiritual insight. But this I do know, that this group, "The Solitude of the Soul" is the work of the Spirit within this man. And his work carries a deep spiritual message to those who are ready to receive it. And in years to come this message will be understood by thousands, for everyone who receives it to-day. This work shall live long after its maker has forsaken the earthly body that he now uses as an instrument. It will live because it carries a message—because it conveys a mighty truth.

Jerry And The Bear

The Law's plan of developing an individual—Folly of clinging to old worn out sheaths—The story of Jerry and the Bear—Who Jerry was—He meets the Bear—The fight—The result—The consequences—The change in Jerry—The moral.

The Law, in its efforts to develop Man into a self-reliant being—into an individual—first tries the simpler plan of bringing a steady pressure to bear in the direction of gradual progress and growth, impelling the man to think and act himself into a more positive condition each day. After a while the man, feeling behind him the steady push of Life, and being conscious of the attracting power of the Absolute drawing him to higher things—leading him up the mountain path of Attainment—learns to trust the propelling and attracting power, and, ceasing his resistance, moves along in the direction of gradual unfoldment and growth. He casts off sheath after sheath—and grows. He does not attempt to impede or interfere with his development, but cheerfully and joyfully presses forward to his unfoldment. He finds pleasure in each stage, and should pain manifest itself he knows it as the growing pains of the child—a promise of greater things.

There are some, however, who seem determined to cling to their old sheaths, and resist the pressure of growth to the utmost. They are unable to withstand the steady pressure, and the attracting power, carrying them forward, and their resistance brings them much pain and friction, and they are pushed this way and that by the pressure of the growing Self, resisting and struggling all the time. The Law has several ways of dealing with these people, for their own good, and often, with a supreme effort, tears them from the surrounding sheath to which they are clinging and forces them into a broader and wider life, against their wishes and in spite of their struggles and cries.

Many of us, looking back over our past lives, smile as we recognize how we were forced into new fields of work and endeavor—how we were broadened out in spite of ourselves—how we were torn from our old surroundings and environments, in spite of our lamentations, reproaches, and cries, and placed amid new scenes and faces. This thing is repeated over and over again, until we learn the lesson and cease to be unduly attached to persons and things, and become willing to yield ourselves to the onward moving force and co-operate with the Law instead of opposing it.

Many men and women who steadily refuse to stand erect and assert their independence, are deliberately worked into a position where they *must* declare their freedom from the things upon which they have been leaning, and are forced to stand up and face conditions from which they have shrunk all their lives. The Law has a way of picking up those shivering mortals who stand around the river's edge, and throwing them into the stream, bidding them to strike out and SWIM. It prefers the easier way of teaching you to swim by degrees—of acquiring knowledge by easy stages—but if you refuse to learn in this way, it will resort to the vigorous plan just mentioned—but swim you *must*, one way or the other.

I am going to tell you a story—not a particularly pretty one, but one that will give you an idea of what I mean, and how the plan works. It's about animals—but many a truth has been conveyed by fables in which animals were the actors, and this homely little tale from the wilderness may convey to your minds the point of this talk better than do my words. Here's the story:

Once upon a time a man, away up in one of the Northwestern States, owned a dog named "Jerry." He was not very much on looks—and less in good qualities. He was not of any fancy breed—just Dog, that's all. He had drifted on to the farm from Somewhere and had been kicked and cuffed around in his early youth, until he was afraid to claim a right to live at all. He grew up into a worthless animal—snapped at by smaller dogs—bullied by those of his own size—looked down upon by all. He expected to be kicked by everybody in sight—and, of course, got kicked. (Men and dogs who go around expecting to be abused, always draw upon them the thing they fear and expect.) His tail seemed a magnet which attracted all the tin cans around that neighborhood. Pitying did not seem to do him any good—it only made him more miserable and abject than ever, just as it acts in the case of some people. The poor chap gradually dropped down to the lowest state of dogdom, and his case seemed hopeless. The farmer would drive to town every once in a while, and Jerry would sneak along under the wagon, in manner seeming to apologize for taking up even that space. His appearance would be the signal for all the dogs of the several farms along the road to chase down to the wagon, rout him out, and roll him over in the dust, the performance being repeated at every farm to and from the town. The farmer, at last, feeling that the dog was bringing his establishment into disrepute, and knowing that "Hopkins' Jerry" was becoming a township jest, determined to put an end to the animal's unhappy career. But Destiny intervened—possibly in order to give me a tale to point the moral of this talk—and to give you something to remember in trying circumstances.

Jerry strayed away from the farm one evening, being chased a part of the distance by some of the smaller dogs who delighted in bullying him. He traveled some distance from home and entered the woods. Bear tracks had been discovered in that region, and some of the boys had dug a pit, baiting it with some choice tid-bit pleasing to his bearship, and covering it over with a thin roof which would yield to a light weight. Jerry started across the roof, and in he went. Some hours after a young bear came sniffing around, and he, too, dropped in the pit. Then the trouble commenced.

The bear feeling infuriated by his unceremonious drop, reached out for Jerry and gave him a scratch which caused him to yell. The bear, seeing that there was no fight in his opponent, chased him round and round the pit, until it seemed only a matter of a few minutes more until the dog would be relieved of his misery. Things took an unexpected turn, however. The bear knocked Jerry over on his back, and began giving him the finishing touches. This seemed to bring to life the last remaining touch of self-respect left in the poor brute, and with a mighty effort he sprang straight at the bear's throat and gave him a bite in which was concentrated all the repressed bites of a lifetime. The bear, with a roar, sprang back to the other side of the pit. It was hard to tell which was the most surprised of the two, the bear at the sudden courage of his opponent, or Jerry at the fact that he could fight bear. The dog's self-respect and confidence went up nearly to par. The bear's caution adjusted itself accordingly. After a bit the bear cautiously worked his way over toward Jerry, but the dog snarled fiercely and showed his teeth. They had several rounds before things quieted down, and each time Jerry showed his mettle, and although he was badly scratched he had bestowed upon the bear several tokens of his valor. His self-respect and confidence was now an assured thing, and the bear treated him with considerable deference and consideration. After matters adjusted themselves, the bear and the dog each retired to their respective sides of the pit, and declared a truce.

In the morning the boys came to the pit, shot the bear and lifted Jerry out and carried him home. His tail was several inches shorter, and one ear was missing, and his body was scarred and scratched like the face of a Heidelberg student, but away down in his heart he felt good—and he showed it. The farmer, feeling proud of the animal, carefully nursed him until he was able to move around the house, and then allowed him to go out of doors. As soon as he appeared the other dogs made a rush for him, but something in his look caused them to keep at a safe distance, and they contented themselves with barking at him and keeping out of reach. He did not seem anxious to fight, but he had that look of confidence in his eyes that kept them where they belonged. He had ceased to fear. His tail no longer drooped between his legs, but was held aloft as is the tail of every self-respecting dog. And somehow, that tail did not have the attracting power for tin cans that had formerly marked it. The boys recognized that Jerry had advanced in the scale, and there was something about him that they liked and respected.

About ten days after the dog got well, the farmer took a trip to town, and Jerry accompanied him, trotting along in an unconcerned manner, alongside, behind, or any other place that suited him. As the first farmhouse was reached the dogs came rushing down to have some fun with our friend. They pitched into him as of yore. Something happened. The pack ran yelping back to the house for surgical attention—and Jerry trotted on just the same. This scene was repeated at every farm along the road, Jerry repeating the object lesson each time, finishing up his task by rolling into the dust the big bull terrier in front of the postoffice, who, heretofore, had been the terror of the town. The homeward trip was a triumphal progress for the dog, and all his old foes vied with each other in tail-wagging and other demonstrations designed to let Jerry know that they were proud to be his friends. But he paid little attention to them—he had developed into a canine philosopher. After that he led a happy life. He was not seeking fight, but no boy or dog seemed to seek fight with him. He had cast out Fearthought. He feared nothing that walked on legs. HE HAD MET BEAR.

Now, some of my critics will call the attention of their readers to the fact that I am advising fight. Not so, good friends. I am using this dog story as an illustration, and am trying to show you how the Law will sometimes force a man into tight quarters in order to bring out his courage and self-confidence. It knows the man "has it in him," and it proceeds to use vigorous methods to bring it out into action providing, always, that the man has not developed it before. When a man has been placed in a position where he faces the worst, and is compelled to grapple with the bear, he finds that he has reserve force within him of which he never dreamt before, and he puts forth all his energy to save himself. He finds that when he boldly faces the difficulty the difficulty seems as much afraid of him as he had been of it. He gains more confidence, until at last he beats off the foe, and rests secure in his own strength. He finds that to the man who has abolished Fear and who can smilingly face any situation, Fate is very respectful and obliging, although to the man who fears it is a tormentor. In proportion to a man's fear will be his troubles. When he reaches the position when he can laugh in the face of Fortune, he will find her ceasing her coquetries and falling desperately in love with him.

And after the man has met the great difficulty—fought the mighty fight—he finds that he has ceased to fear the little troubles and trials of life—he feels his strength—he knows his source of power. He holds his head erect and breathes in the pure air of heaven, and feels the warm blood tingling through his veins. He has found himself. HE HAS MET BEAR.

The Unseen Hand

The consciousness of the hand—When it first was felt—Always there—Now as the hand of a father—Now as that of a mother—A lover—A brother—Always guiding—Always leading—A mystery—Some day we will know the owner of the hand.

I have felt the Unseen Hand—have been guided by it—have felt the kind but steady urge in the direction which it knew to be best, though my Intellect failed to see the beauty of the road toward which the Hand was directing me. For a time I rebelled against the impertinent interference of that which seemed to be a thing apart from me—a meddler—an unasked for helper. I had emerged from the dependent state—the state in which I thought it necessary to lean upon others. I gloried in my independence—my freedom—my ability to stand alone. Finding that it was good to stand alone—reveling in the joy of my new found freedom—rejoicing in the fact that the I AM within me was a reality—feeling within me the ecstasy that comes from the recognition of the reality of Individuality—I resented any interference from outside. But the pressure of the hand was still here—it would take my unwilling fingers within its own and lead me on—and lead me on.

Finding that I could not get rid of this unseen helper—realizing that it was intent upon guiding me in spite of my repeated assertions that I was able to take care of myself—that I was big enough to walk alone—I began to study the Something that was so determined to take an active part in the affairs of my life—I started in to become acquainted with it.

I found that it had always been with me more or less, but that I had not before recognized its presence. So long as I felt that I was not able to stand erect upon my feet—so long as I feared—so long as I failed to recognize the I AM—I was scarcely aware of this invisible helper. But when I began to realize what I was—what was my place in the Universal order of things—what were my possibilities—my future—the presence of this unseen hand began to be manifest. When I at length threw off the last fetter that had bound me—when I threw back my shoulders and drew my first free breath—when I shouted aloud with joy at my freedom and strength—when I realized the power that was within me and at my command—when I started out to accomplish that which my awakened mind told me was possible of attainment—when I started to do these things *all by myself*—then I felt for the first time the firm clasp of the unseen hand.

Now gently guiding—now leading—now kindly restraining—now giving a gentle urge toward people, things and conditions—now drawing me back from the edge of a precipice—now directing toward a better path—now giving me a gentle, firm pressure to reassure me of its presence when I doubted—now allowing me to rest my weight upon it when I felt tired—always there.

At times this hand has placed before me conditions that seemed to me to be anything but good. At times it has brought me pain. But I have learned to trust it—have learned to trust it. The conditions that have seemed to me to be undesirable have brought me to desirable things. The pain that I have suffered has brought me pleasure. The experiences that have come to me I would not wish to part with—the more pain, the more experience; the more experience, the more knowledge.

I have learned to love this hand. And the owner of the hand seems to feel and return this love, and now and then, by a sympathetic little clasp, lets me know that I am understood. This hand sometimes seems to be that of a Father—strong and firm—leading on with a confident air. Again it seems to be that of a Mother—gentle and kind—leading me as does the mother lead her child. Again it seems as the hand of a woman who loves me—clinging and warm—neither leading nor being led—just moving on clasped in mine—no words—but with a perfect understanding. The owner of this hand seems to combine within itself the qualities of both sexes—seems to have within itself all the attributes of Father, Mother, Lover, Brother, Sister. It seems to respond to the human need, in every direction. It seems always the hand of Love—even while giving me pain.

I have never seen the face of the owner of this hand. I have never looked into its eyes. I have never seen its form, if form it has. But I have been conscious, at times, of being lifted up in its arms and being pressed close to its breast. I have felt the impulse of the child, at such times, and have felt for the breast of the mother, and have been conscious of the answering mother pressure as I was drawn up close to the body of the owner of the hand. And, at times, have I felt rebellious at the confining clasp, and have struggled and have even beat against the breast with my puny fists as I insisted that I be released from the clasping arms. But, mother-like, the owner of the hand only drew me closer to the breast until I could feel the very heart-throbs within the mother-body—could feel the vibrations emanating from its life—could feel the warm breath upon my cheek as the invisible face bent over me impelled by the mother love.

Again, it takes on the father-form, and I place my little hand within it, and feeling like the boy whose father is taking him on a journey, I say "Lead Thou me on," and go cheerfully and with faith into new lands—new surroundings—new fields. Why should I fear, have I not hold of my father's hand? And the hand at such times rests upon my shoulder, every once in a while, and I realize that the father feels a pride in his son, and sees him growing in strength and knowing—that the father looks forward to a time when he will be able to talk with the boy who will then have grown in knowledge, and will be able to understand some of the secrets of Life that the father will then unfold to him.

And, still again, the hand is that of the loving woman who is walking along the path of Life with the man she loves. It is a tender clasp—the fingers tingle with love—the arm presses close to mine. I hear no voice—no words are needed—soul talks to soul in the silence. We walk on and on and on. We understand.

And, still again, the hand seems that of a brother—a twin brother. Neither the protection of the father—the loving tenderness of the mother—the thrill of the lover's touch—is there. I feel not that the hand is that of a stronger being—I am conscious only of the brotherly clasp—the touch of comradeship—the presence of an equal. I feel by my side a helper—someone who will back me up in time of need. And I stroll along by his side and laugh with joy. The joy of the boy is again mine. The joy of companionship is again mine. And, lo the hand of the brother seems to grow—he and I are again men. And something in his hand-clasp seems to say to me, "Come, brother, let us go forth into the unknown future. Let us have Faith. There are lands awaiting our coming. Let us enjoy them. Let us explore them. Let us be filled with the spirit of adventure, and go forth. Let us see—let us feel—let us know." And I return the clasp, and say, "Aye, brother, let us go forth. Whither thou goest there will I go. Thy joys shall be my joy—thy pain my pain. Let us go forth—let us go forth to the Divine Adventure."

And, so, manifesting the attributes of all human relations, in turn, and at the proper time, the owner of this unseen hand is near me. I feel his presence—I am aware of his nearness. At times faith grows faint, and I think it all a delusion—a phantasm—a dream. All seems lost, and I weep. But, lo! in the midst of my despair, I feel the hand upon my head—I know that it is a reality and, through my tears, I smile.

Shall I ever know the owner of this hand? Shall I ever see its face? Shall I ever understand the mystery of its existence? I know not. But faith whispers in my ear, "Wait! All is well! When the pupil is ready the Master appears. When your eyes have a clear vision and can bear the sight, then shall you see the Face of the owner of the hand. You have entered the Path and there is no turning back. Go on—go on in Faith, Courage and Confidence. Why should you doubt—have you not felt the pressure of The Hand?"

Aye, why should I doubt or question? Have I not felt the pressure of the Unseen Hand? Open your hands, friends, that the Hand may clasp yours as it has mine. While your hand is clenched in Anger and Hate—while it clutches tight the gold it has snatched from the hand of another—while the fingers are drawn together with Fear—it cannot receive the Unseen Hand. Open it wide—reach it out—offer it in friendly clasp—and you will feel within it the touch of that which you seek.

The Unseen Hand is waiting to clasp yours. Give it welcome—give it welcome.

How Success Comes

Seeking success through mental powers—Holding the thought alone not sufficient—How to get the real benefit of thought-force—Fall in with the workings of the Law—Stand on your own feet—One step at a time—"I Do" as well as "I Am."

Many of the men and women who have been seeking Prosperity by means of the powers of the mind, have done so by "holding the thought," and then folding their hands and calmly waiting for some "lucky" event to happen, or in other words, for the long sought for prize to drop down into the laps, from out of the Nowhere. Now, I have heard of a number of cases in which things apparently came about in this way, although I have always felt that a little investigation would have shown some good and natural cause behind it all, but as a rule the law does not work in this way—it does not leave the old beaten road of cause and effect. It is no Aladdin's lamp which has merely to be rubbed in order that glittering gems, and showers of gold, be poured out into the lap of the owner, as he lies back on his cushions, lazily rubbing the lamp with the tip of his little finger. The law expects from the man who would invoke its mighty aid, a little honest work on his part.

I think that the majority of those who have met with a greater share of Success by means of the wonderful power of Thought, have met with such Success not by having it fall from the skies, but by following out the ideas, impulses, yes, inspiration, if you will, that have come to them. The man who has turned his back upon the old negative Mental Attitude—who has turned his face toward the rising sun—who has allowed the voice of Faith again to be heard—who knows that the Law which rules the motions of the worlds and still takes note of the sparrow's fall, has his interest at heart and asks but for Faith—that man, I say, finds that from time to time ideas will come into his mind just when they are needed; will find that the Law takes cognizance of all human needs and has prepared a way to satisfy them. He finds that new ways are pointed out to him—avenues of escape from unbearable conditions—signboards pointing out the right road, but he must have FAITH in these little hints from the Infinite, and must follow them. The Law will open the door to you, but will not push you in. And when it finds that you refuse to see the open door, it softly closes it, and not until many weary years have passed do you recognize what you have missed. And the Law insists upon doing its work in its own good way—not in *your* way. You may know what you want, but you may not know just the right way to get it, although you think you do. The Law will give you many a hint, and many a gentle push in the proper direction, but it always leaves you the liberty of choice—the right to refuse. It does not insist upon your love, your Faith; that is, it does not *make* you love and have Faith, but until you *do* love and have Faith you are not conscious of the promptings of the Spirit, or, at most, dismiss them as beneath your notice. Oh, ye of little Faith, when will ye learn.

The man who understands the workings of the Law, acts upon the tender impulses imparted to him, without resistance. He does not ask to see the end of the journey, but he sees the step just ahead of him very plainly, and he hesitates not about taking it. He does not expect the Law to bring RESULTS and place them in his hand. All he asks and desires is that the way be pointed out to him, and he is willing and ready to do the rest himself. The true man or woman does not wish to be fed with a spoon. All they ask is that they may have a fair chance to reach the source of supply, and they can manage to handle the spoon themselves. If any man think that the Law is an incubator of parasites—of leeches—of vampires—he is greatly mistaken. The lesson of the Law is to teach every man to stand upon his own feet—to lean not upon another—but at the same time to feel that he is guided by the great Law of which he himself is a part, which manifests within him as well as without him, and that, consequently, while placing his trust in the Law, he trusts in himself. Not paradoxical at all, when you have the key.

Yes, yes, the Law expects every man to do well the work that lies to his hand—and to do it well, whether it is irksome or distasteful or otherwise; and as soon as he ceases to rebel and beat his wings against the bars of the cage, the way is opened for the next step; and if he does not take that step, he must work away until he learns to take it. And so on, and on, the lesson of each task to be learned before the next is presented. Work? why certainly you must work. Everything in the Universe works unceasingly. When you learn to look upon work as a joy and not a curse, then you are beginning to see your way out of the grinding process. Then you are getting a glimpse of the Promised Land. Why bless your hearts, Work is the best friend you have, the only trouble is that you have treated it as an enemy and it has paid you back in your own coin. When you learn to treat it as a friend, it will be only too glad to make up, and you will get along like two old cronies.

Now, you people who have been sitting with folded hands and "calmly waiting," and complaining that your own has not come to you, listen: You are mistaken. Your own has come to you—that's just the trouble. Your own is the thing you attract, and you have been attracting just what has come to you. Start in to-day, determined to fall in with the workings of the Law, and pay attention to the "I DO" side of things as well as the "I AM," and you will receive new light. Great things are just ahead of you, but you must reach out for them—they're not going to drop into folded hands. This is the Law.

The Man With The Southern Exposure

Southern exposure as good a thing in a man as in a room—The man who faces the sun—Lives one day at a time and does the best he knows how, and is kind—Finds Joy and carries it to others—Simple, loving, kind—Open yourself to the sun.

Did you ever go house hunting? Then you remember how the agent laid much stress on the fact that certain rooms had a "Southern Exposure." No matter how many other good qualities the house had, all was subordinated to the fact that the best rooms faced the South—had the longed for "Southern Exposure." The very words conveyed to your mind the sensation of balmy breezes—the freedom from the rude blasts of the North—the cheering rays of the Sun—plenty of light and healthful vibrations coming from old Sol. Ah, that "Southern Exposure"—how much the words convey.

Now, if this "Southern Exposure" is such a good thing in a room, why isn't it a good thing in a man? Did you ever meet the man with the "Southern Exposure"—the man who faces the Sun? Do you recall how he brought with him the inspiring Solar vibrations? Do you remember how the wrinkles and frowns disappeared from the faces of those in his presence? Do you remember how, long after he had departed, the memory of his presence cheered you—the thrill of his thought vibrations remained to stimulate? We all know this man with the "Southern Exposure," God bless him. We couldn't get along without him. There are a number of him, and he is scattered all over the globe. We call him by different names, but he is always the same man. After we have felt the cold Northern chill emanating from some of the cold, despondent, negative people with whom we have come in contact, what a relief it is to meet some one who carries with him the mellowing sunny, vibrations of the South wind—the man with the "Southern Exposure." As the vibrations of the Sun bring life, energy, and strength to all things having life, so this sunny man brings positive, bright, cheerful and happy thoughts to us, and stimulates, encourages and strengthens us. He actually radiates sunshine and cheer in all directions, and thaws out the natures that have become well nigh frozen from contact with people of the other type. Oh, it's a great thing, this "Southern Exposure" in a man or woman.

This man faces the Sun. He is an optimist. He looks on the bright side of things, and gets all there is in Life—he LIVES. He manages to extract "fun" out of the most unpromising conditions and things, and goes on his way with a smile, and a cheerful song, an abiding faith in the Absolute. He lives his life, one day at a time, loving all of God's creatures and letting the creatures know it—carrying a message of hope, and courage, and a helpful suggestion to all mankind. He is the salt of the earth, and Life would lose its flavor if he were taken from us. And how smooth the pathway of Life seems made for him. It matters not in what station he may be placed—what seemingly small degree of material prosperity may come to him—what may be his surroundings and environments—he makes the best of everything—he still catches the rays of the Sun, and rejoices—he has the "Southern Exposure."

He is broad and tolerant—merciful and forgiving—devoid of Hate, Envy and Malice—free from Fear and Worry. He minds his own business, and grants you the same privilege. He is full of Love, and radiates it to all the world. He goes through Life in his own sunny way, meeting cheerfully the things that drive others to Despair and Misery—somehow things seem to be smoothed out for him, and he passes over the stony road, unharmed. His Peace comes from within—and all who meet him feel his presence. He does not *seek* after friends or love—Friendship and Love come to him as a right—he attracts them. People are glad to see him come, and sorry to see him go. Little children and animals are drawn to him, and know him as their friend and lover. He is as much at home in the tenement of the laborer as in the palace of the wealthy—both places seem home to him, and their occupants on a level. Brother to both Saint and Sinner is he, and he loves one as much as the other, for he somehow feels that each is doing his best. He looks for the good in the Sinner—not for the sin in the Saint—although he knows that both exist. He is not a Pharisee—he recognizes within himself all that is within both Saint and Sinner—he knows that he is not without sin, so he dares not cast the first stone. The outcast recognizes in him a brother—the woman who has passed through the fiery furnace trusts him and is not afraid, for she knows that he understands. He, being near the Sun, knows that it shines alike on Saint and Sinner—he feels that when God withholds his Sunbeams from his most disobedient child, then may he withhold his love from his most degraded brother or sister. Until that time comes he sees fit to love them. He does not Condemn—he lets God exercise that prerogative, if he sees fit—he does not feel fit to act as Judge. He believes that the Universe is conducted on sound business principles—that God knows just what he is about and does not require any gratuitous advice from Man.

He works, and works well. He finds Joy in his work—pleasure in the humblest tasks. He likes to Create things—and he is proud of that desire, for he feels that it is an inheritance from his Father. He does not seem to hurry—nor is he rushed. He has plenty of time—Eternity lasts a long while, and he is in it NOW. He is not afraid of Death—or even Life—he knows them as one.

He goes about his way—doing his best—and letting the other fellow alone.

He has an abiding Faith in the Absolute—he believes in Infinite Justice and Ultimate Good. He does not fear his Father—he cannot find room for Fear where Love abides. He does not believe that there is a bottomless pit into which his loving Father intends to plunge him—he has too much confidence in his Father to think that. He believes that there is enough Hell on earth to burn away the mistakes and ignorance of Man. And he believes that all the burning ones will eventually emerge purged of their dross. He knows that his Father is near him, for he has felt the pressure of his hand. In the darkness of the night he has felt the Father's presence—by the glare of the lightning flash he has seen His form, for a moment, and that memory is burned into his brain. He faces the Sun—this man with the "Southern Exposure."

He is Simple, Loving, Kind. He is of the Elect. He is a prophecy of the Future. And he is on the increase. On the Tree of Life are many promising buds, which the Sun of the Spirit is nursing into beautiful blossoms that will yet fill the world with the delicious fragrance of Love.

There are certain people who have come into our midst silently and without announcement. They have found places waiting for them. They have come to prepare the way for their brothers and sisters who are in the womb of the future—they are working quietly to prepare a home for their unborn brothers and sisters when they come. They are the forerunners of the Coming Race. Smiled at—sneered at—persecuted—reviled—pitied—it matters not. God has sent them—they have his message to deliver—that's why they are here. The world may raise its eyebrows—shrug its shoulders—tap its forehead significantly—but these new people smile, they know, they know. They see the misunderstanding multitude as mere babes in the Spiritual knowing—many of them babes unborn—and they heed them not.

Take notice of these people—they are making their presence felt. They are wielding a silent powerful influence, and are molding public opinion far more than are the blatant reformers, the boastful leaders, the bespangled figures strutting at the front of the stage. The people who are thus being used—instruments in God's hands—are these quiet men and women who are facing the Sun—these people with the "Southern Exposure."

If you feel the call to join the ranks of these people—do not resist, but answer cheerfully "I hear; I obey; I come." Allow the seed to grow into the plant, the plant to put forth leaves—bud and blossom. When you feel the impulse, do not resist—open yourself to the Sun—receive its vibrations—and all will be well. Be not afraid—have within you that Love which casteth out Fear—place your hand in that of the Absolute and say "Lead Thou me on." After long ages of wandering, you are coming Home.

A Foreword[1]

An individualist—Wearing no ticket or label—No one has a corner on Truth—Enough to go around—The Infinite Power back of all things—The Real Self is Spirit—The Law of Attraction—Fearthought—The Brotherhood of Man.

*** * I generally call myself a Mental Scientist, and am so known to my friends, but I merely use the term because it is broad and comprehensive, not because I bear the ticket of any particular school of the New Thought—not because I wear the badge of any special leader. I am an Individualist. I believe in the right of every man to think his own thoughts—to find his way to the Truth by whatever road he may see fit, even if he prefers to cut across fields in getting there. I believe that whilst all men are brothers, and each a part of a mighty Whole, still each one must stand squarely upon his own feet—must work out his own salvation—must do his own thinking. I believe that Truth is everywhere—in everything, and that we may uncover a bit of it wherever we may happen to dig. I do not believe that any person has a corner on the Truth—a monopoly of Knowing. I do not believe in Popes, in or out of the New Thought. Each of us will uncover his own little bit of the Truth, but we must not imagine that we have the Whole Thing. There's enough Truth to go around—and to spare.

I believe that there is an Infinite Power in, and of, all things. I believe that, although to-day we have but the faintest idea of that Power, still we will steadily grow to comprehend it more fully—will get in closer touch with it. Even now, we have momentary glimpses of its existence—a momentary consciousness of Oneness with the Absolute. I believe that the greatest happiness consists in maintaining toward the Absolute the attitude of the trusting child, who, feeling no doubt of the parent's love—no doubt of his wisdom—places his little hand in that of the parent, and says:

---

[1] An extract from the article of this name in which the author introduced himself to the readers of the magazine "New Thought," upon assuming the position of co-editor, in December, 1901.

"Lead Thou me on." I believe that he who feels towards the Absolute, the trustfulness of the babe which places its little tired head close to the breast of the mother, will also be conscious of the tender answering pressure, as the babe is drawn just a little closer to the mother heart. I believe these things—I have felt them.

I believe that Man is immortal—that the Real Self is Spirit, which uses mind and body as its tools, and manifests itself according to the fitness of the tools. I believe that Man is rapidly growing into a new plane of consciousness, in which he will *know* himself as he is—will recognize the I AM—the Something Within. Many are having glimpses of the Truth every day—the first glimpses of the light of the great Dawn are even now being perceived by those who are awake and watching.

I believe that the mind of Man contains the greatest of all forces—that Thought is one of the greatest manifestations of energy. I believe that the man who understands the use of Thought-force can make of himself practically what he will. I believe that not only is one's body subject to the control of the mind, but that, also, one may change environment, "luck," circumstances, by positive thought taking the place of negative. I know that the "I Can and I Will" attitude will carry one forward to Success that will seem miraculous to the man on the "I Can't" plane. I believe that "thoughts are things," and that the Law of Attraction in the thought world will draw to one just what he desires or fears.

I believe that Fearthought is the root of more misery, unhappiness, disease, crime, failure and other undesirable things than any one thing in the world. I intend to attack this monster most vigorously, through these columns. I intend going for him with the grace of God in my heart, and a good hickory club in my hand. I will cause many of you to tear out Fear by the roots—you don't need it about you. I will preach the gospel of Fearlessness. There is nothing in the world (or out of it) to fear except—Fear.

I will also preach the gospel of Backbone to you—will insist upon your inserting a steel-rod vertebra in the place of that india-rubber affair that some of you are carrying around with you. You doubt this, do you?—well, just you wait and see.

I believe in the Brotherhood of Man. I believe in being Kind. I believe in everyone minding his own business—and allowing everyone else the same privilege. I believe that we have no right to condemn—"let him who is without sin cast the first stone." I believe that he who Hates, is an assassin; that he who Covets, is a thief; that he who Lusts, is an adulterer; that the gist of a crime is in its desire. Seeing this—looking into our own hearts—how can we Condemn? I believe that Evil is but Ignorance. I believe that "to know all is to forgive all." I believe that there is good in every man; let us help him to manifest it. I believe in the absolute equality of the Man and the Woman—sometimes I think that the odds are slightly in favor of the Woman. I believe in the Sacredness of Sex—but I also believe that Sex manifests on the Spiritual and Mental planes, as well as on the Physical. And I believe that to the pure all things are pure.

I also believe in the gospel of work—in "hustling." I believe in the I DO, as well as the I AM. I know that the man who will take advantage of the Power of the Mind, and who will manifest that power in action, will go forward to Success as surely and as steadily as the arrow from the bow of the skilled archer.

Partnership

Next to marriage, partnership is the most important association—Mental partnerships—Be careful whom you choose as your mental partners—Get into partnership with the best thoughts—Dissolve partnership with the other kind—"I Can, I Will; I Do, I Dare."

Next to marriage, a partnership arrangement is the most important association into which a man or woman may enter. Its consequences are far-reaching and difficult to escape, and to a very considerable extent one is bound by the acts of his partners. This being the case, it is of the utmost importance that one should exercise the greatest diligence and care in selecting partners. If any of my readers were to contemplate entering into a partnership agreement with others, he would be sure to select those who were possessed of the most desirable qualities, and those most conducive to success. He would carefully avoid those possessed of Lack of Confidence, Fear, Worry, Discouragement and others of the "I Can't" class. He would seek out the Courageous, Confident, "I Can and I Will" men. He would keep away from those in whom Hate, Malice, Jealousy, Envy, Bigotry and other traits of Ignorance were strongly manifest. He would, in short, choose those who possessed to the greatest possible degree the qualities most conducive to Success and would as carefully avoid those possessed of opposite qualities. There is no doubt of the truth of what I have just said—every one of you will admit it.

Now, I do not purpose telling you about business partnerships of the ordinary kind—you know all about those—but I will call your attention to the fact that you are every day forming partnerships of a most important character and far-reaching in their effects, but of which you probably have been unaware. When your attention is once called to the matter, many things will seem clear to you that have heretofore appeared quite dark, and you will be able to avoid mistakes, in the future, that have been quite common in the past. This is an important lesson, and I trust that you will give heed to what I say.

I have stated, in previous articles, that your mind is a mighty magnet, attracting to itself the thoughts emanating from the minds of others. Like attracts like in the world of Thought, and the prevailing character of your thoughts will be manifested in the character of thought waves drawn to you from the great ocean of thought. Your thought mingles and coalesces with thoughts of a corresponding nature sent out from the minds of others, and both you and the other senders are strengthened in the mental attitude by reason of the joining of forces. *You are entering into a mental partnership* with those unknown thinkers, and attracting them to you, and you to them. Why do "birds of a feather flock together," in business and everyday life? Simply because they are irresistibly drawn to each other by the Law of Mental Attraction. The people with whom you are brought in contact are those of the same mental key as yourself. You may not agree with this statement, but a close analysis will prove it. The pushing, "hustling," wide-awake man will attract to himself thought-partners of the same stamp, while the man who is afraid is always sure to find himself surrounded by people having the same defects. And not only is this true in the sense that the Law brings you into actual contact with people of the same mental key, but you are connecting yourself with hundreds of others who are thinking along the same lines, although you may never actually come in physical contact with these people. You are going into partnership with them, and will share in the firm's profits and losses, just as you would in case of an ordinary business partnership. And it is easy to foretell upon just what side of the firm ledger the balance will appear.

When you approach a man on business, with your mind laden with thoughts of Fear, Lack of Confidence, etc., you strike a similar keynote in that man, and he instinctively feels that he has no confidence in you or your business, and if he is a man whose predominant note is Courage, he will feel the inharmony and get rid of you as soon as he can. If, on the contrary, he is also a "I Can't" man he will feel a fellow feeling for you, but it will do you no good; it will be a case of "misery loves company," and the first thing you know you will find yourself and that man in an earnest conversation about "dull times," "poor crops," "the country is going to the dogs," "no chance for a man nowadays," "we're all going to the poorhouse," etc., etc. I've seen it happen many a time, haven't you?

But if you are an "I Can and I Will" man, and he is the same, see how different things are. He will warm up to you and will feel that he understands you, and sooner or later you and he will do business with each other, in fact, the arrangement is begun with your first meeting. If you can get yourself in something like the same mental attitude of a man with whom you wish to do business, you will get along with him, never fear.

When you have something in mind upon which you are working, and you are at the same time maintaining the proper mental attitude, you are placing yourself in psychic touch with every other man in the same line who is holding the same mental attitude. You draw inspiration from them, and both parties to the mental partnership share in the profits. Both will share, to a certain extent, in each other's progress and both will draw largely from the mental stock of those who are working along the same lines, but who are holding a negative mental attitude. In fact, the whole store of knowledge and progress along those lines will be tapped by these partners holding the positive mental attitude. New plans, ideas, combinations, schemes, devices will spring into being in their minds, and they will not only help each other, but will draw upon the less positive people. This seems a hard law, but it is like all of Nature's laws, so severe that we are forced sooner or later to learn the lesson. We learn by experience only. This operation of the Law of Mental Attraction is a good example of one of the meanings of that saying, so dark to many: "To him that hath shall be given; to him that hath not shall be taken away, even that which he hath." At any rate, that is the way the law works.

And it is not only in the matter of Success that this mental partnership works. Its operations are manifest everywhere. You will notice that the negative emotions draw to themselves people, thoughts and things upon which they can feed. Let a man or woman manifest Jealousy, and, lo! as if from the earth spring apparent causes for that jealous feeling. All sorts of things seem to conspire to feed "the green-eyed monster" into a state of fatness. And let a man or woman get a notion that people are trying to "slight" them, and let them continue to hold this thought, and it will soon seem to the poor victim of Fearthought as if everybody in the world was determined to snub, slight and tread upon him and hurt his feelings. If he persists in this attitude, life will become a burden too heavy to bear, and there will be no possible relief for him except a change of mental front. Let one imagine that everyone is trying to cheat him, and he will be a lucky man if he does not find that the things he feared have come upon him. Let a man cherish thoughts of Hate and Malice, and sooner or later he will become involved in all sorts of hateful, malicious schemes and occurrences, with his partners whom he has drawn to him. "He who lives by the sword shall die by the sword," is proven every day. He who thinks every man is a rogue will see enough rogues to justify him in his belief, and will probably end up by having people think of him as a rogue—he will draw all sorts of roguish people, things and circumstances to him.

Did you ever start in the morning feeling cross and crabbed? Well, if you did you probably found that after the inevitable domestic row over the buckwheat cakes and coffee—after you had left your wife with tears in her eyes, and the children in good shape to get into trouble in school—that everyone seemed to "have it in for you." Some fellow in the train seemed to deliberately tread on your pet corn, another jostled you, and so on. When you got down to business, everything went wrong, and unless you brought yourself up with a short turn you had a dreadful time of it all day, and were glad when night came that you might sleep it off. You will always find that there are plenty of people waiting to go into mental partnership with you in such cases. If you are looking for fight, you will get it.

I tell you, friends, that people are all more or less in psychic touch with each other, and the sooner we recognize this fact the better it will be for us. This Law of Mental Attraction works either good or bad for us, according to the uses we make of it. If we run contrary to the law we will be taught lesson after lesson, until we learn something. But if we fall in with the workings of the law we will reap the benefits that come to Man when he masters and controls any of Nature's great forces.

Now, don't make partnerships of an undesirable kind. If you do you will have to bear the consequences. If you have already formed such a partnership, dissolve it at once and go into liquidation. After a while you will have cleared up the old debts and straightened matters out and will begin to do business on another basis. And I want to tell you right here that you can get into the best mental firms in the world if you only go about it right. They will not object to you if you are a fit member, and, in fact, they could not keep you out even if they wished. The doors will open at the magic touch of the spoken word backed up by the proper mental attitude. Cut loose from the old thought associations and form new connections. Get in touch with the right kind of thought-waves, people and things. Cultivate the proper mental attitude and demand an entrance to the firm you wish. Good men are scarce in all branches of business, trades and professions. There's room for you—away up at the top, too. Get what belongs to you; do not be cheated out of your heritage. Assert yourself. Join to-day that good, hustling firm, whose name on the signboard reads: "I CAN, I WILL, I DO, I DARE."

The Seekers

The secret of life—The riddle of existence—Sought now as ever—The whyness of things—Attempts to answer the riddle—The Seekers—Fantastic creeds and queer philosophies—Revamping old ideas—The story of the man and the stars—The answer to be found within the soul.

"I laugh at the lore and the pride of man,
At the sophist schools and the learned clan,
For what are they all, in their high conceit,
When man in the bush with God may meet?"

—Emerson.

Man is trying to reason out now as in the past, the secret of Life—the riddle of Existence. He seeks to know from whence he comes, whither he goes, and what is the object of his existence. He wants to know the *whyness* of things—what it all means. He is like the squirrel in the cage, which exhausts itself in traveling the long road of the wheel, only to find itself at the end of its journey just where it started. Or worse still, like the newly-caged wild bird, he dashes against the bars of his prison, again and again, in his efforts to regain his freedom, until at last he lies weak and bleeding, a captive still.

It has ever been so, from the childhood of the race until the present time. Sages, seers, prophets and philosophers have endeavored to reason out the problem, but their labors have availed nothing, and the riddle remains unanswered. Man has traveled over and over the circular road of thought, only to discover that it has no beginning—no ending. He thinks that he has explained things, but he has merely given them names. All the scientific research, all the theological and metaphysical speculation, has failed even to explain the sprouting of the mustard seed. Life and Death is a mystery to the most brilliant man of this civilization, as it was to the ignorant creature of the stone age. Races, nations, civilizations rise and fall; creeds are born, grow strong, weaken and die, but the secret remains a secret still.

The present day seems to have reawakened the latent desire of man to see behind the veil. The pendulum which carried so many thinkers to the materialistic extreme is beginning to swing in the opposite direction, and is causing a strange and wonderful revival of ancient creeds and philosophies. Those who have long since turned their backs upon the accepted creeds now find themselves in the company of those who still claim allegiance to the church, but who feel themselves cramped by the creeds fashioned for them by their fathers.

The leader of the New Thought, reaching the top of the mountain, often finds himself face-to-face with a scientific *savant* who has reached the same place by climbing up the other side of the hill. And the scientist and the New Thought man need not be surprised to find a leader of advanced religious thought claiming a foothold on the top of the same hill. But the trio, after they have congratulated themselves upon reaching the summit and ending their journey look around them, and lo! their mountain is but a foothill, and far above them, towering higher and higher, rise range after range of the real mountains, the highest peaks being hidden among the clouds!

One has but to look around him to see how strenuous has grown the search for the answer to the riddle. New creeds, philosophies, cults and schools confront us at every turn. The past has been ransacked for its discarded philosophies, which have been renovated and trimmed anew for modern use. The dust has been brushed off many an old and almost forgotten creed, which is pushed to the front under a new name and with new trimmings. Plato is worked overtime to furnish the twentieth century creed promoters with material to be done over. The wildest dreams of the ancients are toned down a little, and boldly offered to the eager multitude as the long sought for solution of it all. Priests and teachers of all the religions of all lands are among us vying with the priests and priestesses of the new philosophies and creeds of our own land, and bidding for public favor. And these new home-made philosophies, how frightfully and wonderfully are they made! The old philosophies of Greece and Rome are skilfully dovetailed with the creeds of the Orient, and the result is a thing differing from anything ever seen before by gods or men.

Brahmins, Buddhists, Confucians, Mahommedans and Sun Worshippers claim thousands of followers in our land, and Isis and Osiris will before long again be given a place and duly installed in the new Pantheon. Thor and Odin will doubtless be revamped, and the rites of the Druids revived. We are looking every day for the arrival on our shores of the advance agent of the Joss propaganda from the Celestial kingdom.

And the home product is, if possible, more fantastic and *bizarre* than the imported article. The wildest claims and statements are made with an air of authority, and are accepted as "gospel" by the adherents of the several sects. One does not know whether to sigh or weep as he watches some of the modern prophets and prophetesses strutting their little stage and cutting fantastic capers before high heaven, thus adding to the gayety of the nations. The demand for these things has been created, and nothing seems too highly spiced for the devotees of the latter day creeds.

And the followers of those strange prophets, what of them? Many of them are mere excitement hunters; others that class of people possessed of a consuming thirst for something new; some are honest seekers for the Truth; and others are those who have cut away from their old moorings and are drifting about, rudderless and without an anchor, at the mercy of any stray current which may sweep them along. There are thousands of people who never heard of the philosophies and creeds of the ancients, who are now dazzled by the revamped doctrines expounded by the modern prophets, and who, being impressed with the strangeness and novelty of the (to them) new truths, accept them as inspired and emanating from the *Absolute*. New gods have arisen and also new devils. The "Malicious Mental Magnetism" of the Christian Scientists is as much a devil to them as was the orthodox devil of one hundred years ago to our forefathers.

The new cults usually begin by performing cures by means of the power of the mind and other natural laws, which they attribute to the principles and teachings of their particular sects. Many of them now, however, frankly admit that they are past the healing stage, and look down upon the mere healing of disease as a thing too nearly allied to the detested "material" plane to be seriously considered. The time of the leaders is now principally occupied in announcing and elucidating wonderful, high, spiritual truths for the seekers, soaring away up in the clouds of transcendentalism, leaving their followers behind, gaping upwards like a crowd at a country balloon ascension.

Once upon a time there was a reformer who attended a public meeting, and took part in an exciting debate on an important question of the day. At last, heated, wearied and disgusted by the fruitless struggle, he left the hall and started for home. It was a beautiful, cold winter's night, and the heavens were studded with stars shining bright through the clear frosty atmosphere. Pausing for a moment in his rapid walk, he glanced upward. The stars were twinkling away merrily. They did not seem to be at all disturbed by what had been going on in the meeting. They appeared just the same as when, in years past, as a boy he had looked at them with wondering eyes. As he gazed, a peaceful calm came over him, and his worry, doubts and fears seemed very petty. At last one little star appeared to notice him, and he thought he could see it cast a good-natured glance downward, saying, in a cheerful voice, "Why so *hot*, little man?"

When we feel cast down with doubt, torn with anxiety, weak from loss of faith, faint with fear, let us look aloft at the stars. When we see those distant points of light, knowing them to be centers of solar systems, knowing that beyond, beyond and beyond are countless other suns and world, let us pluck up a little courage and realize that we are a part of a mighty Law, a stupendous plan. Let us know that the Power which called these things into life, and which is able to manage them, and even greater things, has us in charge and will not allow us to be destroyed. Let us know that we are but in the kindergarten stage of existence and that we shall go on and on and on, from plane to plane, ever onward and upward in the scale, until at last we shall be able to spell out the lines of the primer of Life, and learn the multiplication table of the Universe.

Let us in the meanwhile live on in trust and hope; one day at a time; living our own lives; doing our best work; getting the joy which comes from the simple, human life; lending a helping hand. Let us abolish Fear and Hate, and replace them with Courage, Confidence and Love. Let us look for Good rather than Evil. Let us know failure as merely a lesson in Success. Let us look upon Death as Birth. Let us do the best we can with this world, knowing that the next world will find us prepared for its task. Let us know that we are in Eternity right NOW. Let us know that God is not so far away as we have been taught, for is it not true that in Him "we live and move and have our being!"

Let us preserve our sense of humor—for it will guard us against many a fear, many a folly, many a delusion.

And, finally, let us keep out of the throng which is rushing wildly hither and thither, after leaders, prophets, sages, seers. Let us look within ourselves and see the little flame which burns steadily there. Let us know that we have within us the Light of the Spirit which naught can extinguish. And let us say with good old Newman:

"Lead, kindly Light, amid the encircling gloom
    Lead thou me on.

The night is dark, and I am far from home;
    Lead thou me on.
Keep thou my feet; I do not ask to see
The distant scene; one step enough for me.
    Lead thou me on."

Mental Pictures

"I hang bright pictures in my mind"—Bright pictures encourage one; gloomy ones depress—Get rid of your old gloomy mental pictures—Make a bonfire of them—Get rid of the particularly miserable one, first of all—Then put bright ones in their places.

"I now hang bright pictures in my mind," said a friend to me, recently. Her remark explained to me without the necessity of further words, the cause of her bright, cheerful and happy disposition, so greatly in contrast with that of the despondent, fretful woman I had known a few months ago. The change seemed so remarkable that one would have almost expected her to have claimed some startling occurrence as the cause of the wondrous transformation, instead of giving so commonplace an explanation.

But just think how much there is in this thought: "I hang bright pictures in my mind." Stop a moment, and let the thought sink deep into your inner consciousness. "Bright pictures in the mind," why not, indeed? If we wish to make a chamber, or office, bright and cheery, we see that nothing but pictures representing bright, cheerful subjects are hung there. They may be the choicest engravings or paintings, or they may be some little inexpensive things, but just so they are bright and cheery the purpose is accomplished, and the room somehow seems a happier, more joyous place than before.

If we were preparing a new room for the occupancy of some dear one, would we place there any but the brightest picture? Would we hang there pictures of pain and misery, hate and murder, jealousy and revenge, sickness, suffering and death, failure and discouragement? Would we do this thing I ask you? Would *you* do it? And if not, why not, pray? Simply because you instinctively feel that the gloomy, hateful subjects would react upon the loved one. And you know, is the same way that the bright, cheerful, inspiring subjects are likely to uplift, stimulate, encourage and make better the occupant of the chamber.

Have you ever noticed that some rooms always seem to exert a beneficial effect upon you, while others seem to depress you? Certainly you have. Well, the next time you go into these rooms, look around a little and see if the explanation of your moods is not to be found in the character of the pictures on the walls. You may not have specially noticed them before, but your sub-conscious mental faculties have taken up the impression, and the reflex action has affected you. Who can resist the "fetching" qualities of a bright, baby face, smiling from a little picture on the mantel, or on the wall? Not I, for one. And who can help feeling the sense of comradeship for the kindly St. Bernard whose great, affectionate eyes look down upon you from the engraving on the other side of the room. And on the other hand, who could—but, now I'm not going to describe the other kind of pictures in this article.

But now to get back to the "pictures in the mind." If the gloomy pictures on the wall affect people, what do you suppose will be the effect of carrying around gloomy, fearful, hateful, jealous, envious, despondent mental pictures? Can any good come of lugging this trash around with you? Come, now, be honest. Why don't you bundle up these horrible chromos of the mind, and then make a bonfire of the lot. Now is the time for a mental house-cleaning—get to work and clean out these miserable daubs, and replace them with nice bright, cheerful, happy, sunny, mental works of art. Do it to-day. You can't afford to put it off until to-morrow—indeed you can't.

Oh, yes, I know that you have grown attached to some of these old mental pictures—you've had 'em around so long that you hate to part with them. There's that particular miserable one at which you're so fond of looking—you know which one I mean. You see, I know all about it. You've been in the habit of standing before it with folded hands, and gazing, and gazing, and gazing at it. And the more you gazed, the more miserable you grew, until at last you felt that you would like to lie down and die, only that there was some work to do around the house, and you couldn't spare the time. Yes, *that's* the picture I mean. Take it down and put it on top of the bonfire pile, and touch off the whole lot. Then go back into the house and hang up all the new ones to be found, and the brightest one of the lot must hang in the place of that dear old miserable one that you threw out last—that one which was so hard to part with (the meanest one in the lot, always).

And after you have done these things, how good you will feel. See how bright and cheerful the sun is shining; how pure and fresh the air seems—

take a good long draught of it; look out the window and see the fleecy white clouds floating across the sky; the sky itself—how blue it is; and just listen to the bluebirds down by the old gate—Spring must be coming. Ah, how good it is to be alive!

Don't Retail Your Woes

A miserable habit—It grows as it is fed—A nuisance to friends and neighbors—It brings to you more of the same kind—You will get what you look for—Looking for trouble brings it—Don't imagine that you are being "put upon"—Don't retail your woes.

Don't retail your woes. Do you think that it does you any good to go around with a long face, telling your tale of woe to everyone whom you can induce to listen to you? Do you think that it does you any good? Do you think it helps you to overcome your troubles, or makes your burden any lighter? No, I don't believe that you think any such things. All your experience teaches you that people do not like to listen to long-drawn-out tales of your troubles—they have enough of their own. Even those who are always ready to lend a helping hand and to give what aid they can to one who needs it resent being made targets for a continuous fusillade of troubles, woes, griefs, etc. And you know very well that a constant repetition of your own woes will only make them seem greater and more real to you. And then the chronic retailer of woe grows to be like the journalist—develops a keen scent for matter to be dished out to others—she needs it in her business. When one gets into this habit of carrying about tales to her friends, she runs out of ready material, and eagerly looks around for more with which to supply the demand. She becomes quite an adept at discovering insults, sneers, double-meaning remarks, etc., on the part of her friends and relatives, where nothing of the kind was intended, and she rolls these things over and over in her mind like sweet morsels before she serves them up with appropriate trimmings, to her listeners.

You will notice that I say "her," in speaking of the victim of this demoralizing habit, and some of my readers of that sex will undoubtedly take me to task for blaming it on the woman instead of the man. Well, you all know my ideas about the equality of the sexes—about their being different, but one being as good as the other, with the odds a little in favor of the woman. But I feel justified in saying that this habit is one that seems to have a special liking for women, and it generally picks out a woman for its victim in preference to a man. When a man acquires this habit, he becomes such a nuisance to his friends and associates that sooner or later he will notice that they avoid him, and the chances are that some blunt fellow will tell him that he has no time for listening to tales of this kind, and that if he, the complainer, would display the same energy in attending to his business that he does to peddling around tales about how badly he has been used, he would not need any sympathy. But woman, God bless her, does not like to hurt the feelings of others in this way—she suffers the infliction in silence, and then tells her friends how she has been bored. She will listen to her woe-retailing friend, and seem to sympathize with her, and say, "Oh, isn't it dreadful;" "how could she speak so harshly of you;" "you poor dear, how you must have suffered;" "how could he have treated you so unjustly," and other things of that kind. But when the visitor goes, she yawns and says, "Dear me, if Mrs. Groan would only try to say something more cheerful; she gives me the horrors with her tales about her husband, her relatives, her friends, and everybody else." But Mrs. Groan never seems to see the point, and she adds to her list of people who have "put upon her," as she goes along, her tired-out friends being added to the number, as their patience wears out.

And then the effect upon the woman herself. You know the effect of holding certain lines of thoughts; of auto-suggestion; of the attractive power of thought, and you can readily see how this woman makes things worse for herself all the time. She goes around with her mind fixed upon the idea that everybody's hand is against her, and she carries about with her an aura that attracts to her all the unpleasant things in the neighborhood. She goes around looking for trouble, and, of course, she gets it. Did you ever notice a man or a woman looking for trouble, and how soon they found it? The man looking for fight is generally accommodated. The woman looking for "slights" always gets them, whether the giver intends them or not. This sort of mental attitude fairly draws out the worst in those with whom we come in contact. And the predominant thought draws to itself all the corresponding thought within its radius. One who dwells upon the fancied fact that everybody is going around trying to injure him, treat him unkindly, sneer at him, "slight" him, and generally use him up, is pretty sure to find that he has attracted to him enough people who will humor his fancy, and give him what he expects.

In "Thought Force" you will remember, I tell the story of the two dogs. The one dog, dignified and self-respecting, whom no boy ever thinks of bothering. The other dog, who expects to be kicked by every passing boy, and who draws himself up, and places his tail between his legs, and actually suggests the kick to the passing boy. Of course he gets kicked. It's wrong for the boy to do it, I know, but the dog's attitude is too much for the nature of the average boy. And "grown-ups" are built upon the same plan. These people who are going around in the mental attitude which invites unkind treatment, generally manage to find someone who will have his natural meanness drawn out to such a convenient lightning rod. And, in fact, such people often generate harsh feelings in persons who scarcely ever manifest them. Like attracts like in the world of thought, and one draws upon him the things he fears, in many cases.

But one of the most regrettable things about this woe-retailing woman, is the effect the habit has upon her own mind and character. When we understand how one is constantly building up character, adding a little every day, and that our thoughts of the day are the material which are going into our character-structure, it will be seen that it is a matter of the greatest importance what kind of thoughts we think. Thoughts are not wasted. They not only go out in all directions, influencing others—attracting persons and things to ourselves—but they have a creative effect upon our own mind and character. Thought along a certain line will develop certain brain-cells to a great extent, and the cells manifesting the contrary line of thought are allowed to dwindle away and shrivel up. Now, when we have our minds fixed upon the thought that we are long-suffering mortals, and that everyone else is trying to do mean things to us; that we are not appreciated, and that those who should care most for us are only biding their time until they can hurt us; we are building up our minds along that line, and we find ourselves in the habit of looking for the worst in everybody, and we often manage to bring it to the surface, even if we have to dig hard for it.

Some of this class of people seem to take a particular delight in bringing upon their head the harsh words and "slights" of others. Now, I really mean this. I have seen people go around with that "I'm a worm of the dust, please tread on me" air, and the same expression as that in the eyes of the dog which expected to be kicked. And when somebody would be nagged into saying or doing something that they would not otherwise have thought of, the woe-seeker's eyes would assume an expression of "I told you so," and "It's only poor me," and "It's all I can expect, everybody wishes to crush me," and a few other assorted thoughts of that kind. And then she will go to her room and moan and weep, and dwell upon her miseries until they seem to be as large as a mountain. And then the first chance she gets she will run around the corner to a friend, and will retail all the new stock of woes which she has accumulated, with fancy trimmings, you may feel sure, and the friend will try hard to avoid showing that she is bored at the tale she has so often heard, but will say nice little things, until the mourner is sure that the whole world sympathizes with her, and she feels a glow of righteous indignation, self-pity and martyrdom. Oh, the pity of it all! These people go through the world, making things harder for themselves, their friends, their relatives, and everyone else with whom they come in contact. They are constantly seeking to keep their stock fresh and attractive, and display more energy in their retailing than the average man or woman does in business.

This thing of looking for trouble is a very unfortunate thing in families. As a rule, I think that woman gets the worst of it in family troubles. The economic position places her at a disadvantage, and she often suffers all sorts of horrible things, rather than have her troubles made public. But I must say that *some* women bring upon themselves all that they get. I have known them to get in a frame of mind in which they could see nothing but unkindness, where the utmost kindness was meant. Man is not an angel—far from it—but the attitude of some women is enough to bring out all the qualities other than angelic. They assume that they are "put upon" and live up to that idea. Every word that the man says is twisted and distorted into something entirely different from what he intended. The mental attitude produces moral astigmatism, and things are seen at the wrong angle. All the little things that happen are promptly retailed to some mischief-making neighbor, who is in the game for the excitement it affords her, and who laughs at the wife behind her back, and talks about her in turn to some third person. And the wife fairly draws upon herself all sort of things that never would have happened otherwise. She knows that her neighbor is waiting for to-day's budget of news, and she, almost unconsciously, shapes things so that the facts justifying the news are forthcoming. Did you ever notice that woman who keeps her troubles to herself does not have nearly as much bickering and strife in her household as the one who has acquired the retailing habit?

Don't retail your woes. Keep them to yourself, and they will die, but spread them, and they will grow like weeds. You are making things worse for yourself—are drawing things to you—and are spoiling your mind, disposition and character by this miserable business of retailing woes.

Life

There is in each of us a potential Something for expression—The Something Within—The plant of life—No use trying to repress it, for develop it must—Life has a meaning—Growth, development and unfoldment—The lesson of life.

There is in each of us a potential Something, pressing forth for expression and growth in the direction of ultimate Good—casting off sheath after sheath in its progressive development and unfoldment—impelled by the impulse imparted by the Primal Cause—attracted upward by the Absolute.

Failing to understand this impulse of the growing Something—seeking relief from its steady pressure—we look upon it as an intruder, and instead of allowing it to develop and grow naturally, we endeavor to kill it, or to train its growth after our own petty notions. We fail to see that this Something is like unto the plant which grows on steadily and surely, from seed to blossom, until its potentialities are fully expressed. We do not realize that this Plant of Life should be allowed to grow as does the lily, freely and without restraint, unfolding leaf after leaf, until the plant stands in its complete beauty, crowned with its divine flower.

We would train the plant into some fantastic shape—dwarf it as the Chinese do the oak, that it may become the pretty ornament of the parlor instead of the noble monarch of the forest. We would have it grow *our way*, not according to the law of its being. We fancy that we know what is best for it, losing sight of the fact that deep down in the subconscious depths of its being reposes that which directs its every effort toward the Good—forgetting that its attraction toward the Absolute is drawing it steadily and irresistibly in the right direction. We forget that the plant will fulfill these impulses so long as there remains in it one atom of life. The seed in the ground will express itself in its little shoot, often moving weights a thousand times heavier than itself in its efforts to reach the rays of the sun. The sapling may be bent and confined to the ground, but its branches, following the laws of its being will instinctively shoot upward. Restrict the growth of the plant, if you can, but, nevertheless, it will move along the lines of least resistance and grow toward the sun, in spite of your efforts.

And so it is with the Plant of Life—the Something within us. We are afraid to allow it to grow according to the laws of its being, but wish to model it and shape it in accordance with the theories of ourselves or others (more frequently the latter, for most of our ideas on the subject are borrowed). We seem to imagine that the Intelligence that thought the plant into existence did not understand its business, and we are afraid that without the assistance of our mighty intellect the poor thing will grow into a misshapen and unsightly thing. We would alter the shape designed by its Maker, and would twist it into the form approved of by the passing fashion of the hour. We would substitute for the beauty and symmetry of Nature, our own fantastic ideas of form.

But, like the plant, this Something of ours will not submit to the confining bonds—will not conform to the false standards which we would set up for it. Submitting as long as it must, it stores up reserve strength day by day and keeps up a continuous steady pressure in the direction of its desire, and some day, by a supreme effort, it throws off the interfering obstacles, and, obeying the laws of its being, again grows toward the Sun.

Life is growth. It moves along, pressing this way and that way, along the lines of least resistance, drawing to itself that which it needs for its complete expression and growth, using this thing and that thing to-day, and discarding them to-morrow, after they have served their purpose—after their helpful qualities have been extracted. It assumes many forms in its growth, discarding sheath after sheath as outgrown. Any attempt to compel it to retain a sheath, which has become outgrown, will cause its life nature to revolt, and, in the end, with a mighty effort, it will burst forth, tearing the confining sheath into fragments. This Something may be restrained temporarily, but its growth is as sure as the rising of to-morrow's sun, and its attempted restraint only results, in the end, in a violent assertion of its right to unfold and develop according to Law.

When we finally come to realize that Life has a meaning—that we are here for a purpose—that the process of spiritual evolution is being expressed in us and through us—that our growth is in accordance with Law—that the Absolute understands its business—then will we cease to attempt to meddle with the Great Plan. We will then cease our futile efforts to mold to our absurd and arbitrary shapes that which is intended to grow in the beautiful form of Nature's designing. We will realize that the power which called into being this Life of ours, knew just what it was about—that this Power placed within that Life the energy which is expressing itself in changing form and color, but which has but one real object—growth toward the sun, and when we realize this truth we will begin to have Faith, and will trust the Law to do that which is best to be done—will realize the folly of imagining that the weight of the Universe rests upon our shoulders. Some of these days we will awaken to the fact that ours is the conceit of the fly resting upon the mighty revolving wheel, imagining that the fanning of his wings causes the wheel to revolve. Some of these times the fly, tired with its exertions, will stop to rest for a few moments, when it will find that the wheel continues to revolve quite well, thank you, without its active assistance. We have been taking our little selves quite seriously, indeed. The Something within is moving steadily and surely toward its goal, and much of the pain of life comes to us by reason of our efforts to restrict it—our efforts to change its motion, direction, speed. It is a mighty aid to those who understand and move along with it—but woe unto those who get in its way and endeavor to obstruct its progress. If unobstructed, there is no friction—if interfered with it manifests friction, which means pain.

This pain is the notice given us by the Law to the effect that we are obstructing the growth of the Life Plant, and, if we are wise, we will heed the warning. By conforming to the growth we will find that there is little or no friction, and life begins to take on new pleasures. By co-operating with the Law, and moving along with it, we will find that things will "come our way" in a most unexpected manner. The Law is a good friend and helper, and is of the greatest assistance to us, if we but trust it to do its work well, in its own good way. We can use its growing force to aid us in our daily pursuits, if we will trust it and move along with it, but we must heed the first sign of friction and understand that we are in some way interfering with its natural growth. By living in accordance with the Law, instead of attempting to oppose it, we will find that we are guided in the direction of places, people and occupations best suited to develop us and to impart to us the experience needed to round out our lives. A realization of this fact by those who have experienced it, has given rise to the saying "nothing ever *happens*." We find the teachers and helpers that we require, and they find us. If we need certain information, we will find it in some person or book, and will thus be placed upon the track of that which we seek.

The Law will sometimes accomplish its results in ways far different from that which we would have supposed to be the best, but after time has passed we can look back and will see that the way by which the results were accomplished was the best possible under all the circumstances. We may meet with some bitter disappointments, losses, sorrows, but in the end these things will be seen as good—will be seen as having been necessary to give us the experience needed—to round out our characters—to enable us to understand.

There are none who would be willing to part with the experience gained from even the most painful events of their lives. After, say, ten years have elapsed no man would be willing to have the memory and recollection of his greatest pain eradicated; if at the same time he would have to part with the experience and knowledge which have come to him by reason of that pain. The pain and its resulting experience have become a part of us, and we are not willing to be robbed of our own.

And we will realize, in looking backward, that if we had been living in accordance with the Law in the past—if we had understood its workings—these very sorrows, disappointments, losses, would have been considered only in view of their ultimate good, and the very sting of the pain would thus have been removed. When we learn to regard the pain of to-day as we now do the pain of ten years ago, we may feel that we are beginning to understand something of the operation of the Law of Good. And when we reach this stage, we will find that the pain is no longer *pain*, but only a form of Good. When we cease to cause friction, friction no longer exists for us.

The lessons of life *must* be learned, sooner or later. It depends upon us whether they shall be forced upon us, in spite of our resistance, with much pain, or accepted by us, understandingly, with knowledge. In one case we will have the pain which comes from opposing the Law; in the other, we will learn the lesson equally well, without the pain of the birching. The *lesson must be well learned in either case*. Choose your method.

Now, I do not wish to be understood as meaning that we should simply fold our hands and wait for the Law to bring all things to us without any labor on our part. Try this way, though, if you like, and see how quickly the Law will rap you over the knuckles to remind you that a task is set before you. The proper way is to take up the task that lies nearest your hand (and some task is *always* there) and do it well, with the knowledge that the task has been placed there in accordance with the Law. If the task is not to your liking, you will know that that is the very reason that it has been placed before you—you have a lesson to learn from it. When the time comes for a change you will find a strong desire for a something else full-grown within you. Now is your chance. Trust to the Law to aid you in working out your desire. The desire is there in accordance with the Law—its very existence is a promise of its fulfillment. With the aid of the Law you will work out your desire. It is true that when you attain the object of your desire, it may not be just what you had thought it—may not be at all what you want. Well, what of that? You have learned the necessary lesson—have lived out the desire and will now outlive it. Something else will take its place. And you will be surprised at the *way* that Law has brought about the accomplishment of your desire. You will learn another lesson in this.

When you have learned to work on, merrily—doing your best—living out each day's life—with Faith and Trust, Confidence and Fearlessness—accepting the development of each day as meaning ultimate Good—seeing and *feeling* that the Law of Good is in full operation—being willing to accept whatever it may bring you—then, and not until then, good friend, will you begin to know what is LIFE.

Let Us Have Faith

Faith necessary in every human undertaking—You have faith in man, but are afraid to trust GOD—The Universe if governed by Law—The Law is in operation everywhere—Don't be afraid—You are a part of the plan—Fall in with the Law—Have faith, have faith.

When you take a journey by rail, you step into the car, settle yourself, take out a book and read, and give little or no thought to the engine or engineer in charge of the train. You go rushing across the country at the rate of fifty miles an hour, with no thought of possible disaster or accident, and for the time forgetting that there is such a person in existence as the engineer. You have absolute faith in the careful management of the road, and in the intelligence of the man who has been placed in the engine. The lives of yourself and hundreds of fellow passengers are practically in the hands of one man, and that man is a stranger to you—you have never seen him—you know nothing of his qualifications—you only know that the management has picked him out to safely conduct you across the country.

You take a steamship to Europe and place yourselves in the hands of a few men who are total strangers to you. You stake your life on their skill, judgment and intelligence. You feel that they would not be where they are unless the management of the line considered them competent. It is all a matter of trust—of confidence. The same thing is true when you take your seat on a trolley car or on the elevated railroad, or even in a stage coach or a private carriage. In each case you place yourself in the charge of another person in whom you have a certain amount of confidence, although he may be comparatively, or wholly, unknown to you.

You place your wealth in a bank, having confidence in its management. You have business dealings with men whom you scarcely know, trusting to their honesty of purpose. In every transaction in life you are compelled to have confidence in people. Your lawyer, your physician, your grocer, your clerks are all taken on faith. One cannot get away from it. If confidence were destroyed the wheels of modern life would stop in a minute. The so-called hard-headed practical man may sneer at Faith, but it underlies every manifestation of the life of this civilization.

Man has faith and confidence in Man, but is afraid to trust GOD. He looks about him and sees millions of worlds, each in its appointed place, each revolving in its own orbit. He has faith that at a certain time each world will be in a certain position, which position may be calculated centuries in advance—but he lacks faith in the Power that created these worlds and keeps them in their places. He has faith in certain Laws—but he doubts the existence of the Law-maker. He sees the wondrous manifestation of Life in great and small. He takes advantage of the telescope and the microscope and explores new regions, and finds the Law in operation everywhere—but he doubts the existence of a great Law which governs his life—his incomings and his outgoings—his great deeds and his petty acts—he fails to realize the truth of the saying that the hairs on his head are numbered, and that not a sparrow may fall unnoticed.

He seems to think that if there is a GOD, he must have made the world and then ran away and left it to take care of itself. He fails to see that Law must govern Man's life as it governs the unfolding of the leaf, the development of the lily. He fails to see that law is in full operation within him as well as without him. He fails to see that as he opposes the operation of Law, pain comes by reason of the friction. He fails to see that the only true philosophy is that which teaches one to fall in with the operations of Law, and to let it work in him and through him.

Do you think for a moment that GOD does not know what he is about? Do you doubt the Supreme Intelligence which knows all things and is conscious of all things? Do you doubt the Supreme Power which manifests itself in all forms of power? Do you doubt the Universal Presence which is in all places at all times? Do you suppose that the manifestation is everything, and the manifestor nothing? Poor man!

Either the Universe is without Law—without meaning—without reason, or it is the manifestation of Supreme and Infinite Reason. Either it is the work of a Demon who sits somewhere and grins and gloats over our misfortunes—our trials—our troubles—our pain—our follies, or it is the work of an All-knowing—All-powerful—All-present Intelligence-Power-Presence which has taken into consideration everything within the Universe, down to the tiniest thing—down to the merest detail. And if this last be true, then everything that happens must be in accordance with Law—everything that happens to us must be the very best thing that could happen to us at that particular time and that particular place.

Things are not run by blind chance—there is Law under everything. Everything has some connection with every other thing—every person has a relationship with every other person. All is One—the manifestations are varied, but there is but One reality. There is a great plan underlying all Life, and Life itself is in accordance with that plan. Nothing ever *happens*. Every occurrence has a bearing on every other occurrence. Chance has no part in the plan—everything is in accord with well ordered laws. There is always an end in view in every thought, word or act. We are constantly being used for the benefit of the whole. There is no escape—and when we get to *know* we cease to wish to escape. He who understands not Law is constantly struggling, striving, fighting and contending against it, and, producing friction, he feels pain. He who understands something of Law ceases to contend against it—he lets it work through him, and is carried along with a mighty force, doing each day the best he knows how, expressing himself in the best possible manner, sailing to the right and to the left, with the wind and against the wind, but still being borne on by the mighty current and resisting it not. He enjoys every mile of the journey, seeing new sights and hearing new sounds—moving on ever. He who understands not, rebels at being swept along—he wishes to stay where he is, but there is no such thing as staying—life is motion—life is growth. If you prefer to pull against the tide—to row up stream—by all means do so. After a while you will grow tired and weary, and will rest on your oars. Then you will find that you are moving on just the same toward the unknown seas, and you will find that it is much easier work rowing or sailing with the current, or from one side of the river to another, than to attempt to stay in the same place or to pull up the stream.

All this fretting—all this worrying—all this contention and strife, comes from a lack of Faith. We may assert fervently that we know that All is Good, and that all is best for us, etc., etc., but have we enough faith to manifest it in our lives? See how we endeavor to tie on to *things*, people, and environments. How we resist the steady pressure that is tearing us loose, often with pain, from the places to which we have wished to stay fastened like a barnacle. The Life force is back of us, urging us along—pushing us along—and move we must. The process of growth, development and unfoldment is going on steadily. What's the use of attempting to resist it? You are no more than a water-bug on the surface of the river. You may dart here and there, and apparently are running things to suit yourself without reference to the current, but all the time you are moving along with it. The water-bug plan is all right, just so long as we do not attempt to stop the current or to swim right against it—when we try this we find out very quickly that the current has something to say about it, and before long we get so tired that we are willing to fall in with the law behind the current. And yet even the opposition is good, for it teaches us that the current is there—we gain by experience. The New Thought does not teach people to stem the current or to swim up stream, although some teachers and some students seem to be of that opinion. On the contrary, the real New Thought teaches us of the existence of the stream, and that it is moving steadily toward the Sea of Good. It teaches us how to fall in with it, and be borne further along, instead of attempting to hold back and become barnacles, or to try to push back up the stream. It also teaches us to live in the Now—to enjoy the darting backward and forward over the face of the waters. It also tells us of the direction in which the current is moving, that we may move along that way, without wasting our energies in trying to go the other. It teaches us co-operation with Law, instead of opposition to it.

Why do we not have Faith? Why do we not see the great Plan behind it all? Why do we not recognize Law? As we have seen, we place our confidence in the engineer of the train—the pilot—the captain—the coach-driver, and the other guiding hands and yet we hesitate to trust ourselves in the hands of the Infinite. Of course, it makes no difference to the Infinite whether or not we repose trust in it. It moves along just the same, guiding and directing—steering and regulating speed—it minds not our doubts and obstructions any more than does the great driving-wheel mind the fly who is perched upon it and who does not like the movement and attempts to stop it by spreading out its wings and buzzing. The great wheel of the Universe is moving around, steadily and mightily. Let us go with it. And while we are going let us spare ourselves the trouble and folly of the buzzing, wing-spreading business.

Let us part with Fear and Worry. Let us cease our imagining that we can run the Universe better than the engineer who has his hand on the throttle. Let us cease imagining that GOD needs advice on the subject. Let us stop this folly of saying "Poor God, with no one to help him run things." Let us trust the engineer. Let us have faith—let us have faith.

Do It Now

> Do to-day's tasks now—Don't try to do to-morrow's work to-day, but be sure and do the day's work Now—The baneful effects of procrastination—Not fair to yourself—Demoralization attendant upon putting off things—The world looking for people who can do things Now.

If you have anything to do—do it. If you have any task to perform to-day—do it Now. If the matter cannot possibly be performed to-day, stop bothering about it, and get to work doing the things of to-day. But don't get into that miserable habit of putting off things until later in the day, or later in the week—do them *now*. The old proverb: "Procrastination is the thief of time," is true, but it does not go far enough. Procrastination is not only the thief of time, but the thief of energy—the thief of efficiency—the thief of success.

We have had much to say about living in the Now—about not dwelling in the past or fretting about the future. And all this is true, and I will probably say it over and over again during the year, because I believe in it, and wish you to get acquainted with the idea. But living in the Now does not merely mean the thinking of the thoughts of to-day—the carrying of the burdens of to-day—the meeting of the problems of to-day. It also means the doing of the WORK of to-day.

To attempt to carry last year's burdens—or next week's burdens—to-day, is folly of the worst kind, as you well know. But it is equally foolish to put off to-day's work until to-morrow. It's not treating to-morrow right—not giving it a chance. The Self of to-morrow is not exactly the Self of to-day. That is, it has grown a little and is the Self of to-day plus the added experience of the day. And it is just as selfish for the Self of to-day to attempt to throw his burdens upon the Self of to-morrow as it would be for you to attempt to throw your burdens upon your brother or sister. It is not only selfish, but it is hurtful to you—it impedes your growth. To-day's work is set before you because of the lesson it contains, and if you refuse to accept your lesson, you are the loser. You cannot get away from the task. It will be placed before you again and again until it is performed, and you might as well do it at once, and get your lesson at the proper time, and not be compelled like the schoolboy to "catch-up" in his work. By putting off things until to-morrow, you are simply heaping up troubles for yourself to-morrow, as to-morrow's own work will have to be done as well as your leftover tasks, and the chances are that neither of them will be done properly. There's no sense whatever in this habit of procrastinating. It is folly of the worst kind.

And not only in the immediate effects is procrastination hurtful to one. One of the worst features of the case is the demoralizing effect it has upon the whole mental attitude of the man. It cultivates laziness, indecision, shiftlessness, slackness and many other undesirable habits of thought and action. It manifests itself in numberless ways in the character of the man who has allowed himself to be tangled in it. It impairs his efficiency—affects his value.

Then again, you are really unfair to yourself if you get in the way of putting off things. You never have any time to yourself if you have a number of old matters demanding your attention. The man who procrastinates is never able to spare time for mental improvement, because he always has some old loose ends to wind up—some old tangle to straighten out. And he loses all idea of the value of time—of getting the most out of every hour, every minute. The procrastinator is the veriest drudge—he has his nose to the grindstone all the time. He never has any time he can call his own. He is a slave to his own habit of "laying things aside." Poor man.

I am satisfied that half the failures of life—yes, three-quarters of them—are due to the failure of persons to do the thing Now. Not only because of what they lose directly by this habit, but because of the effect it produces upon their character. The shiftless habit of thought manifests itself in action. The thought and action, long persisted in, will lead to a demoralization of the entire character of the individual. He soon forgets how to do things right. And that is where so many people fail. The world is looking for people who can DO things—and who can Do Them Now.

If you are one of the procrastinating kind, start in at once and get over it. Put up a sign before your desk, your sewing machine, your work-bench, or wherever you spend most of your time, and have these words in big black letters on the sign:—"DO IT NOW!" By carrying the thought of this NOW way of doing things, and letting it manifest itself in action as frequently as possible, you will find that before long your entire mental attitude regarding work has changed, and you will find yourself doing things when they should be done, without any particular effort on your part. The mind can be trained and taught to do things right. It needs a little courage, a little perseverance, a little will-power, but the result will pay you for your trouble. Start in to cure yourself of this bad habit. Start in at once. Do it NOW.

Get In Tune

Marconi's wireless messages—Vibrations reach only the instruments attuned to the sender—The same law in operation on the mental plane—The correct pitch is the thing—Get in tune with the proper vibrations—Get the messages from the best senders.

I have just finished reading an account of Marconi's wireless telegraphy. It seems that when a message is sent from the Marconi transmitter, the vibrations travel in all directions, and not alone in the direction of the person to whom the message is sent. It would seem to the reader, at first, that any instrument, in any direction from the sender, could and would be affected by the vibrations and would take up and record them. But such is not the case, for Marconi finds that he can attune his receiving instrument to a certain pitch, and that the instrument will receive and record only vibrations emanating from a sending instrument attuned to the same pitch. This is true no matter how near the instruments may be to each other, or in what direction they may be from each other. And all instruments, irrespective of number, that may be within sending distance, will receive the message providing they are attuned to the same pitch.

Now just notice how much this corresponds to what we know of the working of Thought-force. People whose minds are attuned to a certain pitch will receive the vibrations from the minds of others whose mental keynote is the same. And if one maintains a high positive keynote, he will not be affected by the vibrations emanating from the mind of another who may have a low negative pitch. The nearer to our pitch the mind of another may be, the more we feel the sympathetic vibrations in our own mind; the greater the difference in the pitch, the less we will feel in sympathy with him. This will account for the instinctive likes or dislikes that many of us experience when coming into the presence of other people. And how soon do people of kindred vibrations seek out and find each other in a mixed assembly. Many likes, unexplainable by any theory of personal appearance, etc., arise from this cause.

And as the Marconi instruments may have their pitch changed, so are our mental keynotes changed from time to time as we adjust ourselves to new conditions—as we grow. This will explain why two people, who at one time seemed to be in perfect attunement with each other, will drift apart until at last they seem to have scarcely a thought or feeling in common, and yet both of them may be good people, really anxious to be helpful to the other.

But this is not the only way in which the working of the Marconi system resembles the workings of the mind. I have often called your attention to the fact that the holding of certain mental attitudes resulted in the attraction to oneself of thought vibrations corresponding to the general character or the thought held in the mind of the person. Let a man be filled with the spirit of Jealousy, and everything seems to feed that feeling. He hears of cases of faithlessness on the part of other persons; every circumstance seems to confirm him in his belief. The actions of the loved one seem doubly suspicious—signs of guilt are seen in every expression, every move. He draws to himself the thought-waves of other minds vibrating on the same pitch—like attracts like. Let a man drop into the Fearthought condition, and immediately he feels the rush of Fear to his mind. Let him cast aside Fear, and attune himself to the Fearless pitch, and he feels an influx of Courage, Fearlessness, Confidence, Energy and other positive thoughts.

And according to the character of your thoughts, will you draw to yourself people calculated to co-operate with you and be of assistance to you. Even things seem to shape themselves to fit in with the keynote you have sounded.

Not only do you attract to yourself people and things corresponding with your mental pitch, but you send out thought-waves affecting others creating impressions upon them. Go into the presence of an "I Can and I Will" man, and, if you are of the same kind, he will instantly perceive it and will be glad to talk to you. On the other hand, approach a man of this kind, with your mind full of "I Can't," and he will be conscious of inharmony and will want to be rid of your presence at once. Be a man with the southern exposure, such as I described to you in another article, and you will find that you will extract and draw to yourself all the sunniness in the nature of people with whom you come in contact. Be a human wet blanket, such as I have described in another article, and you will find that you will get the meanest qualities inherent in the nature of people with whom you come in contact—in fact you will be able to attract only that kind of people who are as musty and unwholesome as yourself.

Get rid of the old negative notes. Start in and cultivate the positive, joyous, active vibrations, until you reach the steady mental pitch of the "New Thought" man. Then will all the negative vibrations pass you by, finding no encouragement to enter your mentality—then will you receive the bright, cheerful, happy, fearless vibrations coming from others who have reached the same plane of thought.

Get in tune—get in tune.

Mental Toxin And Anti-Toxin

A new toxin—The microbes in the thoughts we think—The new anti-toxin—Thoughts may poison—Fear causes paralysis—Hate causes insanity—Fear and Hate have killed their thousands—Gates' experiments—How to overcome the poison of bad-thinking.

In these days of toxin and anti-toxin—of poison in sausages, oysters, canned beef, ice cream—of anti-toxin serums (that often are more deadly than the original toxin) for the prevention and cure of tuberculosis, leprosy, pneumonia, typhoid fever, tetanus, bubonic plague, diphtheria, and the rest of the list, it requires courage to call the attention of the public to a new "toxin," even if at the same time we furnish an anti-toxin that "anti-toxicates."

We shudder at the thought of microbes and bacilli—and thereby attract them to us; we filter our drinking water, after boiling all the life out of it; we develop into microbe hunters, and see poison in everything we wear, eat, drink or breathe. But we overlook the microbes in the thoughts we think. We encourage the enterprising doctor in his giddy chase after the nimble dollar, as he produces anti-toxin serums to order. The poor, broken-down cart horse is worked overtime in producing filthy pus and serum for the serum-maniac to inject into our circulation. But we overlook the pure, harmless, powerful anti-toxin obtained fresh from the cells of the brain—Right Thinking.

That Thoughts may poison, is a well-proven fact. Depressing thoughts interfere with the cerebral circulation, impairing the nutrition of the cells and nerve centers. The result is that the organs and tissues manifest lost or impaired function—loss of general nutrition follows—and a break-down is inevitable. Fear, worry, anger, envy, jealousy, and other negative thoughts, reflect themselves most disastrously in the human system. Fear has paralyzed nerve centers, and turned the hair white over night. A mother's milk has been poisoned by a fit of anger. Fear and Hate—father and son—have produced insanity, idiocy, paralysis, cholerina, jaundice, sudden decay of teeth, fatal anaemia, skin diseases, erysipelas, and eczema. Epidemics owe their rapid spread and heavy death rate to Fear and Ignorance. Epidemics may kill their dozens—Fear kills its thousands. All the brood of negative, fearful, selfish, hateful thoughts manifest themselves in physical conditions. Stigmata or marks upon the body, caused by fear or desire, are quite common in the annals of medical science and psychology.

Professor Gates, of the Smithsonian Institution, Washington, D.C., in his investigation of the effect of mental states upon the body, found that irascible, malevolent and depressing emotions generated in the system injurious compounds, some of which were extremely poisonous; he also found that agreeable, happy emotions, generated chemical compounds of nutritious value, which stimulated the cells to manufacture energy. He says: "Bad and unpleasant feelings create harmful chemical products in the body which are physically injurious. Good, pleasant, benevolent feelings create beneficial chemical products which are physically healthful. These products *may be detected by chemical analysis* in the perspiration and secretions of the individual. More than forty of the good, and as many of the bad, have been detected. Suppose half a dozen men in a room. One feels depressed, another remorseful, another ill-tempered, another jealous, another cheerful, another benevolent. Samples of their perspiration are placed in the hands of the psycho-physicist. Under his examination they reveal all these emotional conditions distinctly and unmistakably." Remember, this is not "the airy fancy of some enthusiastic Mental Scientist," but is the testimony of a leading scientific investigator in the laboratories of the Smithsonian Institution, one of the best known scientific institutions of the world. "Chemical analysis," mind you—not "transcendental imaginings."

Now I have said enough about the toxin and some little about the anti-toxin of the Mind. I might go on for hours, stating example after example; illustration after illustration, but the tale would be just the same. Now what are you going to do about it? Are you going to keep on poisoning yourself and those around you with vile, malignant thoughts reeking with the miasmatic effluvia of Hate—emitting the noxious exhalation of Fear and Worry? Or will you cease being a psychic pest-house, and begin to fumigate and disinfect your Mind? And after getting rid of all the microbes of Fear and Worry and the bacilli of Hate, Jealousy and Envy, open wide the windows of the Mind and admit the bright Sunshine of Love, and the bracing air of Confidence and Fearlessness.

Come, friends, let us get out of this habit of poisoning the air with Fear, Worry and Hate Thought. Let us join the ranks of the Don't Worry company—the Fearless brigade—the invincible, conquering army of Love. Let us be bright, cheerful and happy—the other things are not worth while. Let us be Confident, Expectant, Hopeful and Fearless—these things are winners. Let us be filled with Love for all men—and we will find that Life is one sweet song. Love, Faith and Fearlessness, are the ingredients of Life's great Anti-Toxin. Try it and be blessed.

THE END

www.ingramcontent.com/pod-product-compliance
Ingram Content Group UK Ltd.
Pitfield, Milton Keynes, MK11 3LW, UK
UKHW040318300826
14791UKWH00003B/970

9 789355 840257